Purpose, Process and Future Directio
of Disability Research

STUDIES IN INCLUSIVE EDUCATION
Volume 24

Scope
This series addresses the many different forms of exclusion that occur in schooling across a range of international contexts and considers strategies for increasing the inclusion and success of all students. In many school jurisdictions the most reliable predictors of educational failure include poverty, Aboriginality and disability. Traditionally schools have not been pressed to deal with exclusion and failure. Failing students were blamed for their lack of attainment and were either placed in segregated educational settings or encouraged to leave and enter the unskilled labour market. The crisis in the labor market and the call by parents for the inclusion of their children in their neighborhood school has made visible the failure of schools to include all children.

Drawing from a range of researchers and educators from around the world, Studies in Inclusive Education will demonstrate the ways in which schools contribute to the failure of different student identities on the basis of gender, race, language, sexuality, disability, socio-economic status and geographic isolation. This series differs from existing work in inclusive education by expanding the focus from a narrow consideration of what has been traditionally referred to as special educational needs to understand school failure and exclusion in all its forms. Moreover, the series will consider exclusion and inclusion across all sectors of education: early years, elementary and secondary schooling, and higher education.

Purpose, Process and Future Direction of Disability Research

Edited by

Simoni Symeonidou
University of Cyprus, Nicosia, Cyprus

and

Karen Beauchamp-Pryor
Swansea University, Wales, UK

SENSE PUBLISHERS
ROTTERDAM/BOSTON/TAIPEI

A C.I.P. record for this book is available from the Library of Congress.

ISBN: 978-94-6209-420-8 (paperback)
ISBN: 978-94-6209-421-5 (hardback)
ISBN: 978-94-6209-422-2 (e-book)

Published by: Sense Publishers,
P.O. Box 21858,
3001 AW Rotterdam,
The Netherlands
https://www.sensepublishers.com/

Printed on acid-free paper

TABLE OF CONTENTS

ILLUSTRATIONS

FIGURES

TABLE

LIST OF CONTRIBUTORS

Karen Beauchamp-Pryor is an honorary research fellow at Swansea University, Wales, UK. Following the completion of her BSc in Social Policy, she received a full university scholarship to undertake a PhD, which explored the experiences of disabled students in higher education. Subsequently, Karen was awarded an Economic and Social Research Council postdoctoral fellowship which she used to disseminate her research findings through publication and presentation of papers. Karen recently completed her monograph *Disabled students in Welsh higher education: A framework for equality and inclusion*, with the aim of generating discussion about those barriers that work to exclude disabled students.

Simona D'Alessio is a researcher and a teacher in the area of inclusive education, policy analysis and disability studies in education. Since 2006 she has been working for the European Agency for Development in Special Needs Education specifically focusing upon research and policy analysis activities. In 2008 she completed her PhD in Inclusive Education at the Institute of Education, University of London, UK. In 2011 Simona's findings were published in her monograph *Inclusive education in Italy: A critical analysis of the policy of integrazione scolastica*. She has conducted research in the area of policy analysis, inclusive education and disability studies at national and international levels. As a former specialized secondary school teacher, she has a wide experience in school practice. Simona is the co-founder and editor of the *Italian Journal of Disability Studies*. She is also a visiting fellow at the Institute of Education.

Eleni Gavrielidou-Tsielepi is an associate lecturer of the School of Education at the University of Nicosia and a teacher appointed within special education in Cyprus. She studied at the University of Cyprus (BEd in Pre-primary Education), the University of Bristol (MEd in Education, specializing in Special Education) and the Institute of Education, University of London (PhD in Education). In the past she has served in the position of a pre-primary school teacher, as well as a teacher in special units in primary and pre-primary schools in Cyprus. Eleni has participated in a number of European funded projects and presented her work at national and international conferences. Her research interests include the historical development of special education, the process of policy formulation and policy implementation in Cyprus and the development of inclusive education. Eleni is an active member of associations connected with the promotion of inclusion in the educational context of Cyprus and is currently working towards the co-authoring of an edited book about the pedagogies of inclusion.

Carmel Kelly completed a PhD in Sociology at the Institute of Education, University of London, UK, in 2008. She is also a graduate of the University College, Galway (BA Hons.), the University of Warwick (MA in Applied Social Sciences) and the

University of Westminster (MA in Women's Studies). Her professional background is in social work. Carmel is a disability activist who has also been a welfare rights officer and a lecturer/consultant on social care policies and practices. Her key interests are disability studies, historical patterns and contemporary themes in welfare provision and delivery in the UK. A central focus of her research is everyday welfare practices with particular reference to their power effects and disciplinary character.

Marion Reichart is a lecturer in Law and the Social Sciences at the Open University, a member of Lawyers with Disabilities Division Law Society, and an Associate of the British Institute of Human Rights (BIHR). Shaped by personal and professional experience of disability, Marion seeks to promote respectful inclusion, anti-discrimination and human rights approaches to grass-root, business, government and public sector clients. She has disseminated best practice strategies for the former Disability Rights Commission, given keynotes on the UN Convention on the human rights of disabled people, and presented at Disability Intergroup, European Parliament in Brussels. Originally Marion qualified as an ergotherapist in 1982 in Heidelberg (Germany). She holds a First Class Honours Degree in Law (Thames Valley University, London) and in 2007 completed her PhD *Connecting disability equality and citizenship education* at the University of Greenwich, UK.

Ilektra Spandagou is a senior lecturer at the Faculty of Education and Social Work, University of Sydney, Australia. She has been involved in teacher education in special and inclusive education both in Greece and Australia. She has experience of working with general and special education teachers in the area of theories of inclusive education, and the nexus of policy and school practice. Ilektra's research interests include inclusion, disability, comparative education and classroom diversity. Her publications include the recently published book *Inclusive education: International policy & practice* (co-authored with A. C. Armstrong and D. Armstrong).

Simoni Symeonidou is a lecturer in Inclusive Education at the Department of Education of the University of Cyprus. She holds degrees from the University of Cyprus (BEd in Primary Education), the University of Manchester (MEd in Special Needs and Development) and the University of Cambridge (PhD in Education). Her research interests include the history, policy and practice of inclusive education in Cyprus and in other countries, inclusive education curriculum and pedagogy, teacher education for inclusion, disability studies and disability studies in education. She is actively involved in networks and associations which promote inclusive education issues and she has published widely in international journals. Her publications include a book in Greek entitled *Teacher education for inclusion: From research to praxis* (co-authored with H. Phtiaka). Simoni is the scientific co-ordinator of the website *Tessearae of Knowledge* (www.ucy.ac.cy/psifides-gnosis).

FOREWORD

This is an important, original set of papers addressing a selection of significant issues, conceptions, policies, intentions and experiences, relating to cross-cultural research approaches to disability studies and inclusion.

Editing a collection of papers is a challenging, complex and time-consuming task. Deciding on the themes of the book, providing significant, critical, constructive feedback to the authors, is an essential responsibility of such editorial work. Keeping authors involved in the project, getting deadlines met, making decisions relating to the order of the papers, are also examples of their tasks. Good editing can enhance the overall quality of a book.

This is the first time these two colleagues have worked together as editors of a book. They have taken on their responsibilities in an enthusiastic and serious manner. Each paper has benefitted from their perceptive, detailed comments and support. The overall quality of the book is partly a reflection of the painstaking efforts of their work.

The contributors have provided a refreshingly open, honest, self-critical approach covering a range of features relating to their doctoral research experiences. Their accounts evidence a serious, passionate, sustained commitment to the struggles involved in attempting to increase their knowledge and understanding of what it means to be a researcher in a specific context, investigating chosen topics. Research is viewed as a complex learning process, which involves exciting, developmental aspects of engagements and outcomes as well as those elements of uncertainty, doubt and frustration. Hence, there is an element of messiness to this whole process.

In various ways, the contributors view research practice as a continual process of learning and re-learning. Taken-for-granted assumptions, conceptions and practices, are increasingly subject to critical examination. Change is foregrounded in the pursuit of providing more enabling, liberating, research intentions, relations and outcomes.

Overall, a range of important factors are identified and discussed in relation to the complex challenges that the authors encountered throughout their research endeavours, including: establishing an acceptable focus of the research; constructing the research questions; choosing and engaging with specific methods and methodological concerns; developing an heightened awareness of issues relating to the positionality of the researcher; working through the complex and contentious issues relating to conceptual clarity and theoretical frameworks; social model thinking and its implications for research; learning to think, read and write critically; making sense of the findings; various ethical concerns; relationships with participants and the position and role of the supervisor. The overall impact of these carefully focused and analysed accounts, vividly confirms the quality and degree of the time, emotional and intellectual labour that has been involved on the part of the authors.

FOREWORD

This collection of papers provides a rich source of perceptive, thoughtful, thought-provoking ideas, insights, challenging questions and relevant literature. The editors hope that this volume will inspire and encourage readers to pursue high quality research. I welcome the publication of this volume and believe it should be widely read and seriously discussed, especially by students and supervisors engaged in inclusive education and disability studies, for whom it should be essential reading.

Professor Emeritus Len Barton
Institute of Education
University of London

ACKNOWLEDGEMENTS

We are indebted to those who provided valuable guidance and support (whether as a supervisor, mentor or friend) in our early steps of researching disability. As detailed in our chapters we are appreciative of those academics, researchers and activists who introduced groundbreaking debates about doing disability research, which impacted on our way of thinking about our own research.

The idea of forming a network of early career researchers resulted from the encouragement of Professor Len Barton, and enabled a sharing of views about our experiences of the research process. It was at the suggestion of Len that we decided to develop these ideas and to put together a collection of our papers. We are grateful to Len for his advice and support, and his ongoing encouragement and commitment to our work.

We would like to thank Professor Roger Slee and his editorial board for including our volume as part of the series *Studies in Inclusive Education.*

KAREN BEAUCHAMP-PRYOR & SIMONI SYMEONIDOU

1. INTRODUCTION

The content of this volume stems from the experiences of a network of early career researchers with an interest in researching disability. Each of us had recently completed doctoral research and following the encouragement of Professor Len Barton, we formed an international network to share our experiences about researching disability and to contemplate on the purpose, process and future direction of disability research.

Following the initial exchange of details about our doctoral studies it was evident that whilst our approaches differed and our experiences were varied in researching disability across countries and contexts, we were unified by an underpinning desire to explore ideas about researching disability. We were further unified by being a network of female researchers, although the significance of gender on our research varied. As a network of newly qualified researchers we had much to offer, and to say, about our experiences of researching disability.

We present an open and honest reflection on our experiences as postgraduate students, with each of us considering the factors that influenced the direction of our research and the decisions we reached. We sought to identify our interests, motives and values which underpinned our work and to question whether our beliefs were subsequently substantiated, validated, challenged or changed. Our decisions were driven by a range and combination of personal experience of impairment and disability, and professional experience of working with disabled people. The influence of personal and professional approaches within our research is addressed, along with the dilemmas that this might have caused. As newcomers to the research process we discuss our apprehensions about embarking on doctoral research, together with the anxieties experienced along the way, and importantly the motivation that drove us to complete our projects.

Whilst our research focus varied, the purpose of our research was united in furthering debate and understanding about power relationships and the inequality and marginalization experienced by disabled people. Discussion reflects on barriers of power within politics, policy and practice, and the struggle by disabled people in challenging their exclusion. Therefore, many of the chapters discuss the lack of voice experienced by disabled people and the research purpose being one of enabling unheard voices to be heard in the struggle to inform legislation, policy and practice.

We reflect on theoretical discussions within disability studies and inclusive education research and examine the way in which debates about the meaning of

S. Symeonidou and K. Beauchamp-Pryor (Eds.), Purpose, Process and
Future Direction of Disability Research, 1–6.

disability and inclusion determined or influenced the direction of our work. Of particular significance is our understanding of disability in terms of the medical and social model (Oliver, 1990; 2009; Oliver & Barnes, 2012): the medical model reflecting impairment as individual limitation; the social model identifying disability as socially produced dependency. We explore the influence of discussions about the relationship between individual and societal factors and their impact on our research approach, design and analysis of findings. Moreover, where initial research positions were challenged or changed during the research process, the impact of a different approach or direction on the project is addressed.

The influence of discussions within disability studies about the purpose and process of doing disability research on our work is considered. In particular, the powerful contributions featured in the special edition of *Disability, Handicap and Society* in 1992, which identified the frustration and disillusionment surrounding disability research by researchers and researched. As Barton stated:

> Criticisms of such research included their misunderstanding of the nature of disability, their distortion of the experience of disability, their failure to involve disabled people and the lack of any real improvements in the quality of life of disabled people that they have produced. (1992, p. 99)

The ground breaking articles, within the special edition of the journal, highlighted the importance of developing effective and meaningful research strategies. An edited volume *Doing disability research* (Barnes & Mercer, 1997) continued to challenge traditional and dominant approaches to researching disability and addressed the importance of adopting an 'emancipatory' research process. For those of us with a specific research interest in inclusive education other valuable texts included: *Making difficulties: Research and the construction of SEN* (Clough & Barton, 1995); and *Doing inclusive education research* (Allan & Slee, 2005).

The principles underpinning our work varied and we each address ways in which we were persuaded in the decisions taken about our methodological choices. Discussion reflects on those decisions and the appropriateness of approach, along with any regrets over a particular direction taken. The different approaches provide the opportunity of exploring a wide range of research methods (for example the use of observation and in-depth interviewing), together with supporting strategies (for example in-depth case studies and documentary analysis) aimed at strengthening and validating our research.

We identify and examine some of our experiences throughout the process of analysis, writing-up and presenting data and question how far the data resulted in confusions or conclusions. Moreover, we explore our moral and political position as researchers, and the potential ways it might have influenced the validity of findings. Issues about dissemination and the impact of our findings are also considered. Significantly, we question whether our findings influenced policymakers, professionals, organizations representing disabled people, and disabled people themselves; and whether our research contributed to the empowerment of disabled people. Developing these ideas we share our thoughts and dilemmas about our future research aims and challenges.

At the end of each chapter each contributor was asked to identify two questions which reflect the unfinished business that their research has involved. We acknowledge that there are relevant topics that remained untouched or topics that were not researched at the level each one of us would liked to have researched them. By identifying these questions we hope that we will encourage critical discussion by the readers.

As editors, we recognized the value of openly sharing our experiences as novice researchers with others (whether established researchers or those starting out in disability research). Throughout the process of putting together the chapters we encouraged contributors to move away from 'just' providing an account of their research and findings, to questioning and reflecting on those principles which guided their research, with the ultimate aim of developing ideas about the purpose, process and future direction of disability research. The process of revisiting research decisions is challenging and yet at the same time enlightening and thought provoking. Our aim was to encourage authors to provide a self-critical approach, reflecting on their ideology and contribution to the field. The resulting chapters are varied and consequently focus on the importance each researcher attached to the issues outlined.

In Chapter 2, Marion Reichart presents a thought provoking account as she reflects on important influences throughout her research. Her study was about challenging traditional models of citizenship in professional practice and her aim was to connect disability equality to citizenship equality. Marion has a background of law and human rights in Germany and she critically questioned the role of law and the state, together with social and institutional practice, in enabling and dis-abling individuals. She explains how her understanding of the interrelating of the 'personal' and the 'political' experiences of disabled people deepened during the research and influenced her thought processes. She explores her ideological position and the importance of the social model, human rights and political struggle in her work. She describes the stages which influenced her research decisions and in particular the influences which led her to reach her research questions. From the outset Marion identified the importance of engaging with disabled people in her project and she describes the process of developing a 'mash-up' methodology, which would enable her to reach out to a range of authentic disabled voices (from disabled academics to 'ordinary' disabled people): an approach which often resulted in conflicting and contradictory viewpoints. However, as Marion discusses, her hope was to provide evidence of the inequality experienced by disabled people. During the latter stages of writing-up Marion writes that her insight deepened into 'a way of knowing'.

In Chapter 3, Carmel Kelly provides an open and sincere discussion about her research, which explored disability discourses and disciplinary practices in a local authority care management team in England. Carmel sought to identify whether discursive shifts towards a social model position in political, policy and academic discourses were reflected in everyday practitioner perspectives. She reflects on why she chose this particular project and the important influence of her previous work experience and personal background, along with her ideological position and her interests in sociology, social policy and social work. She reveals an enthusiasm, as well as an apprehension, about embarking on the project. Carmel provides an account of the reasoning behind her research methodology and methods (observation, semi-structured interviews and documentary analysis) and reflects on the appropriateness and benefits of her chosen approach: an approach which deepened her understanding of the multilayered character of care management practices. A range of research problems and ethical dilemmas are shared, and Carmel's frankness offers an insight into the quandaries she encountered: for example, her decision to partial nondisclosure of her own social modellist thinking in order to avoid distancing herself from research participants. Throughout the chapter the complexity of power relationships is evident and her discussion is enlightening in drawing out the issues of researching those who are perceived as being in a position of power. The process of unraveling the 'messiness' of data discussed is insightful, and Carmel's concern about the interpretation and validity of her findings is evident. Ultimately, Carmel's findings identify dominant practitioner views of 'expert' status towards disabled people continue to exist, but hidden by social model and user-centered discourses.

In Chapter 4, Simoni Symeonidou identifies the social model as a 'driving force' in her research journey. Growing up in Cyprus she reflects on the dominance of the medical and charitable focus towards disabled people and how her understanding of disability was later challenged. Simoni trained as a primary school teacher and since has been interested in inclusive education and disability studies research. At the start of her doctoral study she set out to combine both fields within her work. Her research aim was to contribute to the understanding of disability and the disability movement in Greek-Cypriot culture. As her discussion develops she insightfully details the dilemmas the social model brought into her research: for instance in deciding an appropriate research framework and paradigm. Whilst the social model shaped her research interest, she engaged with feminist (personal experience of impairment and disability, and the personal is political maxim) and postmodern/poststructural (culture, history and identity) ideas: an approach which helped her conceptualize the experiences of disabled people and the disability movement in an historical and cultural context. Simoni is clear in her commitment to the social model and reflects on why she decided not to adopt an emancipatory research paradigm. She explores her decision to take a hermeneutical research approach (an approach which enables the researcher to construct meaning through interpreting multiple realities) in an endeavor to provide an account of the experiences of disabled people at both a personal and political level, within the multifaceted cultural and historical context of Cyprus. Simoni identifies a range of concerns during the process of data analysis, writing-up and dissemination and explores her thoughts on completing her research journey.

In Chapter 5, Ilektra Spandagou provides an informative account of the challenges she experienced in completing a comparative and ethnographic study on inclusion in secondary schooling in Greece and England. Her attempt to resolve the difficulties of defining 'inclusive education' illustrate the complexity of researching dominant discourses not only in one country, but two. Ilektra set out to identify the way structures, practices, attitudes and perceptions were defined and interpreted as inclusive/exclusive by her research participants, given a differing socioeconomic, political and cultural context. The way Ilektra conceptualized her study informed her methodological approach, but as she discusses it was the research stages of fieldwork and writing-up which were later to prove influential. Ilektra's reflection on the 'messiness' of the research process offers a frank account of the challenges she experienced and her attempts at resolving a range of dilemmas. An open approach is also reflected in Ilektra's questioning about her political and moral obligations as a researcher.

In Chapter 6, Eleni Gavrielidou-Tsielepi considers the influence and impact of the social model throughout her research approach. Reflecting on her first encounter with the social model (whilst studying to become a pre-primary school teacher in Cyprus), she discusses the way her outlook, views and understanding of disability were challenged: challenges which instigated her desire to pursue research. Eleni felt driven 'to make a difference' in achieving inclusion for disabled children in education and questioned why despite a legal framework supporting the 'rights' of children in Cyprus, an emphasis persisted on supporting the 'needs' of disabled children. Her research questioned the gap between official policy and the implementation of policy in everyday practice and she discusses the influence of Gillian Fulcher in determining her research questions. The decisions about her theoretical and methodological framework are reflected upon and she explores her reasoning in the decisions taken. Her approach of adopting different research methods and techniques (bricoleur), included the analysis of documents, observation of policy processes within schools and semi-structured interviewing: as a result her data proved rich and complex. Reflecting on her findings Eleni identifies the power of the medical model in policy enactment. She exemplifies such power in the way the medical model legitimized professional opinion and influenced decision-making processes.

In Chapter 7, Simona D'Alessio discusses her doctoral study as a process in which her views and understanding about disability and inclusive education radically changed. At the start of her project she believed that the Italian policy of *integrazione scolastica* (school integration) was progressive and inclusive. However, her original assumptions were challenged and as she argues she experienced 'a major shift in thinking'. She was influenced by writers in the field of disability studies and within inclusive education, together with the work of Antonio Gramsci and Michel Foucault. A new awareness of inequalities of power within education and policymaking settings developed, together with a realization that the process of integration and inclusion were very different. Her research objective changed and she sought to identify barriers to participation by disabled students, which were often disguised as inclusive policy. From an original individual/medical model position her project followed a new direction and she details the significance of adopting a social model approach on her decisions about research questions, choice of methods and design, form of analysis, dissemination and impact of findings. Utilizing research findings Simona provides illustrative examples of different approaches from different perspectives. Her powerful account is a battle of contested ideas and assumptions and although Simona discusses her experiences as a 'struggle', she concludes that her research journey proved 'rewarding'.

In Chapter 8, Karen Beauchamp-Pryor reflects on why she felt driven to identify those factors which worked to include or exclude disabled students in Welsh higher education. Drawing on her personal experience of impairment and disability, together with her growing interest in disability policy and politics, she details their influence on her project. Karen explores the underpinning principles which guided her study (principles which included a commitment to: challenging oppression; adopting an emancipatory approach; researching from an 'inside' position as a disabled person; shifting the research focus upwards on to those who influence the direction and implementation of policy and practice; and effective dissemination of research findings) and re-examines her research position. She reflects on the benefits of her approach, together with subsequent dilemmas and regrets, and concludes by questioning whether with hindsight she would have done things differently. Throughout her aim was to develop a framework towards securing inclusion for disabled students in higher education and her research decisions were focused on this aspiration.

The final chapter draws together 'our' stories, reflecting on the purpose, process and future direction of disability research. Compiling the volume has been a new experience for us as editors, but from the outset we shared an enthusiasm and desire to put together the experiences, reflections and ideas of network members. Throughout the process we have provided support to each other, as well as receiving encouragement from the network: support and encouragement which has driven the work to completion.

REFERENCES

Allan, J., & Slee, R. (2005). *Doing inclusive education research.* Rotterdam: Sense Publishers.
Barnes, C., & Mercer, G. (Eds.). (1997). *Doing disability research.* Leeds: Disability Press.
Barton, L. (Ed.). (1992). Introduction. *Disability, Handicap and Society, 7*(2), 99.
Clough, P., & Barton, L. (Eds.). (1995). *Making difficulties: Research and the construction of SEN.* London: Paul Chapman
Oliver, M. (1990). *The politics of disablement.* Basingstoke: Macmillan.
Oliver, M. (2009). (2nd ed.). *Understanding disability: From theory to practice.* Basingstoke: Palgrave Macmillan.
Oliver, M., & Barnes, C. (2012). *The new politics of disablement.* Basingstoke: Palgrave. Macmillan.

MARION REICHART

2. A LIBERATING RESEARCH AGENDA: ON HEARING VOICES AND DEVELOPING A WAY OF SEEING

In loving memory of my beautiful son Aaron
February 21, 1988 – March 17, 2013

INTRODUCTION

...there was increasing anger, hostility and suspicion among organizations
of disabled people that much that passed as 'disability research' was nothing
more than a 'rip-off'. (Oliver, 1997, p. 15)

This paper both tells and reflects upon the story of doing disability equality research.
My research focus is on the subject of disability equality and not on disabled people
as the object of research. Research about disabled people without control by disabled
people is referred to as a 'rip off' by Michael Oliver in the above quote. In this
chapter, I do not provide a full summary of my research, but instead look back at
how a particular way of thinking developed and became a tool in disability equality
research. In particular, I reflect upon power relations and show connections between
personal and political disability issues.

Liberating research starts with an imagination of future possibilities and requires
'emancipated' selves. This chapter offers reflexive biographical sketches of this
process and details how three tools developed and strengthened so as to hear authentic
disability voices over themes of citizenship: the application of a 'personal – political
zoom'; the adoption of social model thinking (*Denkmuster*); and the development of
an innovative 'mash-up' methodology.

My research aim was to connect disability equality to citizenship education (in
the UK). From the outset I aspired to have a transformative agenda (Barton, 2005;
Oliver, 1997) that is relevant to the lived experiences of disabled people (people
with impairments or long-term health conditions) like me. I sought to model ways
to engage with disabled people and to reach authentic disability voices, in order to
provide evidence of the impact and extent of disability inequality.

The research questions did not appear at the start of the project. Initially,
I undertook research in Law, comparing German and British employment legislation
and the responses of different legal systems to the question of equality. I wanted to
know whether disabled women could rely upon the law to protect their employment
rights. I had been interviewing leading disabled women and read copious material
on *Recht und Gesetz*, Acts of Parliament, case law decisions, codes of practices,

S. Symeonidou and K. Beauchamp-Pryor (Eds.), Purpose, Process and
Future Direction of Disability Research, 7–25.
© 2013 Sense Publishers. All rights reserved.

commentaries and legal analyses. However, disabled women seemed invisible in these texts. This invisibility needed to be addressed and in this process, I deepened my understanding of the relationship between the personal and political.

THE PERSONAL – POLITICAL ZOOM

It puzzled me that disabled women appeared to be doubly discriminated yet had no legal recourse. Equality laws were widely implemented and available on grounds of race, gender, religion or belief, even on sexual orientation and gender reassignment, but not for disabled people. In Germany (Forum Behinderter Juristinnen und Juristen, 1995; Hermes, 1994) and Britain (Barnes, 1991) and at a European level (Hendriks & Degener, 1994), disabled people were using research evidence controlled by disabled people's organizations and demanded anti-discrimination laws. Additionally, in Germany, campaigners sought a change in the constitution, so that the non-discrimination clause would explicitly promote basic human rights for disabled people and protect against abuses of state power (Heiden, 1996).

With a professional background in law and human rights I began to ask critical questions about the role of the law and how it shaped, constrained, freed or enabled individuals. This section sketches an example of my early learning about how disabled people fair within legal systems. A socio-legal analysis planted the seeds for a way of understanding of how the law works, of how the law expands and contracts in different economic and political times, and therefore, the influence of law in opening or closing opportunities for disabled people. However, it was not until the writing-up phase of my PhD many years later that a deepening insight crystallized into a way of knowing.

Theresia Degener, one of the disabled lawyers I interviewed, invited me to visit after her first son was born. We discussed many experiences where expectations on women as a mother and as a disabled person intersect. I learned how the German welfare system through its laws and with assumptions about ability and risk, tended to dis-able mothers like her. Theresia is a well known human rights lawyer, a co-author of the original background study to the United Nations Convention (2006) on the rights of disabled persons, professor in law and disability studies and is a legal expert and commissioner in the UN Committee. She was born without arms due to the effects of Thalidomide. Together with her partner and close allies, she had to dissuade overzealous professionals from intervention into her private and family life under the guise of welfare concerns for the child.

During my weekend discussions with Theresia, I discovered that such private endeavors were replicated across impairment categories and reflected a collective pattern of struggle for disabled mothers in Germany (Hermes, 1998; 2002; 2004) and elsewhere. Through these collections of narratives, I was learning a way of hearing voices of disabled parents as they echoed citizenship themes of equality and human rights, of dignity and autonomy, and of the right to private and family life. Narratives illustrate dimensions of citizenship where the personal and political, the private and public, are mutually constitutive: they shape and are shaped by each other (figure 2.1).

8

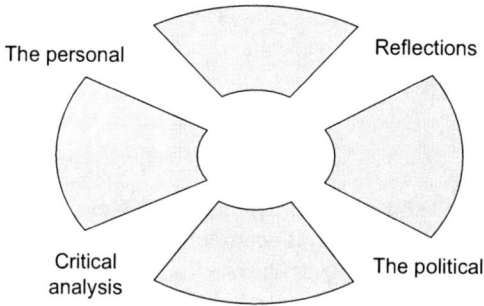

Figure 2.1. Developing a way of seeing: The personal – political zoom (Reichart, 2009).

My understanding of how the personal and political interrelated grew with each encounter and with subsequent reflections upon disabled people's experiences, and thus the personal – political zoom developed into a core research tool. For my PhD I examined citizenship themes of 'equality before the law'. I reflected upon discoveries in the 'personal' sphere of disabled parents, whose children had been taken into care, and critically analyzed the 'political' sphere of the law, where apparently neutral, formal, equal citizenship rights, such as Article 8 of the European Convention on Human Rights (Council of Europe, 1950), collided with the actual experiences of parents classified as having learning difficulties (Case of Kutzner v Germany, 2002). Operating the zoom onto the political aspects showed how the decisions of social welfare and legal professionals ran counter to human rights principles of disabled people. Yet with a personal zoom, parents classified as having learning difficulties were not passive victims, as they challenged the law and dominant social policy. Personal struggles and resistance influenced the political shape of future possibilities, since case law was decided in their favor and at a European level. Disabled parents turned personal issues into collective political action.

Applying a personal – political zoom chimes with the social model of disability (Oliver, 1990; Oliver & Barnes, 2012). As I explored citizenship issues and the curriculum, my thinking was continually challenged by experiences that showed how disabled people in society were not being heard or responded to in any meaningful way. Disabled people were often without basic human rights, and yet there was resistance and struggle. I felt a strong sense of injustice about these situations. It became clear that doing disability equality research meant addressing and redressing injustice. The next section outlines why I decided to examine injustices on the themes of citizenship in the curriculum.

WHY RESEARCH DISABILITY EQUALITY AND CITIZENSHIP CURRICULUM?

The opportunity for this project arose when the University of Greenwich advertised for a PhD studentship, with Michael Oliver (School of Psychology and Social Sciences) as joint supervisor with Christine Lloyd (School of Education and

Training). I give a description in three stages of the tortuous path of my research-student experience that eventually leads me to develop the 'mash-up' methodology: supervision process; ideological warfare; and research questions.

Supervision Process

As each supervisor headed a different department, I was straddling two academic fields from the outset. I must admit, curriculum structures, attainment targets, programs of study, and developments leading to the new National Curriculum in England, were unfamiliar to me. Driven by a desire to enter this new academic world, to prove to myself and perhaps to please my supervisors, academic peers, or colleagues, an internalized pressure to fill my perceived knowledge-gap grew. An expectation to become part of the 'expertise' was dangerous, in terms of research goals with a transformative agenda. At a political level liberating research seeks to redress disability inequality, and at a personal level, the production of knowledge strives to emancipate myself as a disabled person. For years I had immersed myself in curriculum matters, in the very structures and processes that were oppressive, in policy development and education for citizenship debates. The more I did so, the further away I felt I was getting from a liberating disability research agenda, as too much time was spent on institutional or managerial definitions and less and less on the direct experiences of disabled people.

One of the most beneficial aspects of the supervisory process was that as a researcher I must be enabled to think. When I was considering my research question, Michael Oliver probed why I had decided to take this or that direction. He enabled me to reflect upon motivation and feelings, a process which alerted me to any potential compromise or irrelevance. My second supervisor, Mary Stiasny (who was the new head of the School of Education and Training) was invaluable in her guidance on curriculum structures and education policy, and engaged my creativity. In an open and non-judgmental manner she patiently shared my journey of finding a way to hear disability voices.

A good support network of allies was helpful, but so was time to work things out for myself. Both supervisors allowed me (during periods of apparent inactivity) the space to think, to test ideas, engage in dialogue, and the space to heal and recover. Completing my PhD took eight years: expected completion in just three years would have crushed me, as I often needed space to recover my strength from bullish exchanges in oppressive institutional contexts. An illustration of such 'warfare' is given in the next section, where frustrated exchanges left me doubting whether I had any grasp on reality.

Ideological Warfare

On July 2, 1999, I attended a conference in London entitled 'Preparation for adult life: Coherent education for personal and social development?'. Much of the day was concerned with the Secretary of State's proposals for citizenship within the revised curriculum. With a professional background in law and personal engagement in disability politics the potential for raising disability equality issues in the National Curriculum seemed obvious to me and filled me with great excitement.

I was soon struck by the self-evident authority of education professionals and their unveiled hostility to the idea that the conference topics were in any way relevant to disabled people. Delegates, speakers and workshop leaders, head teachers, Local Education Authority advisers, special educational needs co-ordinators (SENCOs), and initial teacher trainers (ITTs), all explained in one way or another that 'special educational need' (SEN) was a 'specialist', separate area. The meaning of my words 'disability equality' were 'stolen, transformed and appropriated' (Eagleton, 1994, p. 187) in a kind of ideological warfare (Allan & Slee, 2008, p. 53). I said 'disability equality' but they heard '*special* needs' or 'SEN' and '*special* educational need'. Disability equality, it seemed, had not (yet) entered the classroom. And when it later did, it often masqueraded as new, when it was a mere use of new words for the same old practices, as Slee explained, practices 'demonstrating a remarkable resilience through linguistic dexterity' (2001, p. 167). What annoyed me most was that delegates expressed concern that everyone wanted to jump onto the bandwagon of citizenship. I was told: 'citizenship teaching must achieve clarity, coherence and manageability'. I felt it loud and clear, the message that disabled people and citizenship in the curriculum did not go together. The uniformity of these messages was stifling.

Of course, 'special educational need' was not my area of expertise. My teaching and learning experience was not as a teacher in the classroom at school, but as a Law and Social Science lecturer at university and as a freelance trainer on diversity issues and social change. In the school context, I worked with Disability Equality in Education to challenge exclusionary practices. I was neither familiar with the various administrative techniques that allocated resources, nor acquainted with the changing role of SENCOs. I had been active with the Alliance for Inclusive Education (ALLFIE), on hearing experiences of parents and young disabled people about these procedures. At university, I was inexperienced in the 'mad, sad, bad' classifications adopted by some colleagues, who offered an overview of special education history to trainee teachers. For me, special education was another way of saying school failure (Barton, 1997) in a historically exclusionary society.

Further ideological battles played out later, when I tested ideas about the history of oppression of disabled people with an international audience of special education professionals (Innovations in Special Educational Needs Support in Regular Education – INSPIRE). The room was full of good intentions, yet low level oppressive rumblings occasionally leaked out. In one of my sessions, as delegates raised the idea that segregated education was akin to apartheid (a particularly sensitive issue, as the discussions took place in the Netherlands), power erupted and closed down any further dialogue.

Research Questions

All of this left me wondering: What was the position of disabled people in society? And who knows? What models of citizenship were there and what did it mean for disabled people? How could my research reduce and change current stifling, oppressive institutionalized patterns and instead lead to effective expression of disability equality in the teaching of citizenship?

Education professionals no longer go about their tasks in tacit acceptance of a diagnostic deficit frame of mind without being challenged. Disability issues entered academic and professional debate in three main domains of research: inclusive education, special education and disability studies. UK law introduced the concept of disability equality: the amended Disability Discrimination Act (DWP, 2005) required public bodies such as schools, colleges and universities, to consult with disabled people, involve them in planning for services and to publish action plans as part of a document called the Disability Equality Scheme (Section 49 A (1) of the DDA, DWP, 2005).

However, there are dangers, as exemplified in the discussion by Oliver and Barton about the impact of feminism:

> The very point when women's studies was accepted as a legitimate academic discipline in its own right was precisely the point at which it seemed to lose its radical cutting edge. (2000, p. 2)

Whilst I believe that disability equality is a long way off from being accepted into the mainstream academic thinking and professional practice, I nevertheless, consider a note of caution is appropriate. Public authorities in education, social housing or health, now speak and write about the 'duty to promote disability equality', but in many cases, it could be argued that they are simply displaying well known linguistic dexterity. At the time of writing, legal changes in the UK threatened to weaken or remove 'disability equality' altogether under the provisions of the new Equality Act (Disability News Service, 2011; DWP, 2010; Gooding, 2010a; 2010b). Patterns of thinking, changing language and conflicting meanings symbolizes a further aspect of the political zoom. My particular *Denkmuster* are outlined in the next section, and the personal is related through further biographical reflections.

IDEOLOGY AND *DENKMUSTER*: FROM THE PAST INTO THE FUTURE

All research is political (Hatch, 2002) and in this section it is important to me to make theoretical and epistemological foundations clear. I will outline my research approach and offer biographical sketches to explore its roots. Critical social theory provided a framework, whilst the main tool for analysis in my research on disability equality was the application of the social model of disability (Barnes & Mercer 2010; Barton & Oliver 1997; Oliver, 1990; 2009; Oliver & Barnes, 2012) to the context of curriculum development and the subject of citizenship (Morris, 2005).

Epistemologically, I drew on and blended a range of traditionally distinct academic fields, with law, education, social sciences, and philosophy. The goal was to construct meaning by examining multiple realities through disabled people's own voices (disabled voices) and positions (disability voices).

The ideological underpinning of my work was rooted in critical social theory. This was originally developed by the Institute für Sozialforschung at the University of Frankfurt in the 1920s. As a form of thinking it had already been familiar, accessible and relevant in my personal and professional endeavors, since I received much of my education in Germany and in the German language. I applied critical theory (Habermas, 1987; 1992; Held, 1992) that integrated political, cultural, economic, structural and psychological aspects of analysis to a discussion of the material disadvantage experienced by disabled people. This approach created a transformative agenda.

In my thesis defense, viva voce, I was asked by Len Barton about how I had encountered the social model of disability for the first time. This was an interesting question upon which to reflect. I concluded that my encounter with the social model was a disturbing, yet liberating experience, and detail my reasons below.

First, I was studying social sciences and enrolled in a module on the changing experiences of women. New concepts and specialist vocabulary challenged me to think in new ways and in a foreign language (English). Professionally, I met Mike Devenney, Dolly Grievson and Dave McDonnell, all of whom contributed to my later research. They were employed in senior roles in the London Borough of Ealing advancing equality and access. Each person was what I call an 'out and proud' disabled role model.

Second, my own impairment effects rarely intruded into the public sphere, and consequently, I was 'passing' as non-disabled most of the time to most people, even to myself. With a condition that fluctuated and was hidden, the social model provided a new way of seeing through which to understand my experience of disability in society. I began to foster an 'emancipated' self, which was able to connect the personal and political. This helped me later to investigate inequalities in citizenship education, such as the fact that only two per cent of the academic workforce disclosed an impairment or health condition.

Third, many years ago my father, Joe Reichart, became a wheelchair user following an accident. He involved me in discussions, cartoons (such as the one presented in figure 2.2 below) and campaigns through which ways of knowing developed. I began to understand, for example, the meaning of rehabilitation laws *Schwerbehindertengesetz*, which were structured around impairment categories and based upon the 'severity of defects'. The law was ostensibly neutral, yet closed its eyes to the material position of disabled people when deciding about the allocation or refusal of appropriate resources, which were necessary to enable independent living choices. I heard the pain in people's voices as they adopted strategies to help them prove that there were simultaneously sufficiently disabled to qualify for support, yet able enough to take an active role as citizens. For some, the 'blame'

Figure 2.2. A cartoon by Joe Reichart. It shows Justicia holding the scales of Justice, but blindfolded. Two disabled people pass, and one stretches his walking stick to reach and lift her blindfold, saying: 'You should open your eyes once in a while'.
© by Marion Reichart

if they failed, too often rested within their own body or personal 'inadequacies': I remember that pain and I remember that anger. *Denkmuster* formed during those times undoubtedly enabled more radical ways of searching out disabled voices: ways that recognized a personal 'internal' zoom that laid the foundations for a critical reading of the law.

Partially shaped by these experiences, I became an ergotherapist at a progressive academy in Germany. Despite the fact, that together with junior doctors we were instructed by some disabled lecturers, most of the teaching remained firmly grounded within an individualized, impairment, deficit model of disability. Abberley (1995) researched the impact of ideology within occupational therapy. He noted that success of client-focused intervention was closely linked to themselves as therapists, whilst failure was often reduced to client resistance. Therapists saw little need to attend equality of opportunity training as they regarded themselves as already progressive in that 'the demands of the disability movement were already incorporated into the theory and practice of occupational therapists (Abberley, 1995, p. 224). Similarly, at the academy I had learned many ways of seeing the therapist as an 'expert' trained to empower the disabled person. The shock and disorientation on discovering the social model of disability as a trained professional was profound and it meant re-evaluating years of knowledge and knowing: professionals do not 'empower', therapists do not 'give' power, but need to 'give-up' power. Disabled people empower themselves.

SOCIAL MODEL THINKING

This section summarizes the social model thinking and outlines three key shifts. A shift from impairment to access was first mooted by Oliver when he changed government research questions, such as 'What complaint causes your difficulty in holding, gripping or turning things?' to 'What defects in design of everyday equipment causes you difficulty?' (1990, p. 7–8). People do not have a disability, but have impairments or health conditions, and are dis-abled by barriers in society, which results in lack of access in the broadest sense and includes access to power. Disability is that experience of exclusion.

Over thirty years after Paul Hunt first read out *The fundamental principles of disability* (Union of the Physically Impaired Against Segregation – UPIAS, 1975), which made the important distinction between impairment on the one hand, and the experience of disability on the other, little progress had been made. The UPIAS principles state that disability is a situation caused by social conditions, which require its elimination; that no one area (such as poverty or education) should be tackled in isolation; and that disabled people should be in control over their own lives. My research findings on themes of citizenship revealed a stubborn insistence on deficit and individual impairments in social policy, rather than access to the citizenship and human rights of disabled people.

In applying the social model, all people (whether disabled people with different impairments or long-term mental or physical health conditions, or non-disabled people who are 'expert' in their traditional well rehearsed systems), are invited to change *Denkmuster* and shift in three significant ways (Reichart, 2007, p. 298):

– Social model: a shift from impairment to access by removing barriers.
– Human rights: a shift from welfare, entitlement or 'special' responses to anti-discrimination and human rights values from the outset.
– Political struggle: a shift away from dependence creating structures, to those created and controlled by, with and for disabled people.

Patterns of thought *Denkmuster* describe interconnected sets of shifts in ideas and beliefs about future possibilities in disability equality and inclusive citizenship. The making of citizenship as an environment of participation and contribution for all is illustrated in figure 2.3, where the expanding circle of self-determination meets access and human rights. Only then can structural change follow and new best practice become embedded, and only then might 'empirical' evidence show how inclusive citizenship works. Only when institutional rules and procedures reflect this shift throughout its practice has the socio-political environment been created for inclusive citizenship. Until then we contest ideologies and until then we struggle.

The model of citizenship emerging from these *Denkmuster* seeks to exemplify an uncorrupted, authentic perspective of disability equality, as inclusive citizenship. Empirically framed case analyses provided the key methodology in this research.

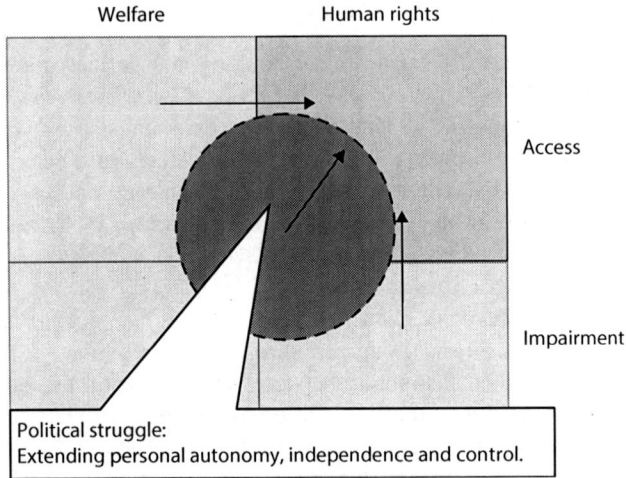

Figure 2.3. Key shifts in social model thinking (image adapted, Adept, 2004).

Overall, I adopted a critical theory stance (Kellner, 2003; Scott & Usher, 1999; Young, 2007), which explored the lived citizenship of disabled people. Unlike the positivist, scientific method claims of neutrality and objectivity, a critical approach recognizes that values, in particular citizenship values, are rooted in 'the personal'. A zoom creates a continuum, in which elements of 'the personal' and 'the political' are simultaneously engaged. This takes me to the third tool in my research, 'mash-up' methodology, which will be introduced next.

MASH-UP METHODOLOGY: ON HEARING VOICES AND CREATING A NEW SONG

In applying a personal – political zoom, it was important to me to explore the authentic nature of disability equality by listening to the voices of disabled people themselves, by unscrambling traditional ideas, examining new perspectives and ways of thinking about disability as shaped by the disability movement in Britain and worldwide. However, disabled people's voices are polyphonic, discordant, and international. It became clear that the sound these voices made was not always comfortable, and by no means concordant: they could be most disagreeable to the unfamiliar ear (figure 2.4). Several questions emerged: Whose voices should be heard? How could they be found? And who should learn to listen?

In an effort to connect disability equality issues to citizenship education, and bearing in mind the demands of 'practical outcomes' for teachers of citizenship, I decided to focus on engaging with mostly freely available, accessible authentic voices 'of' disabled people. Researching disability equality does not mean having

> **SUBJECT:**
> The global voice 4 inclusion
> e-Petition to no 10
>
> **MESSAGE:**
> "We the undersigned petition the
> Prime Minister to: (i) That the UK
> Government fully supports Article
> 1 of The Universal Declaration of
> Human Rights1948 and that all
> citizens have a right to be treated
> with dignity; and (ii) That this right
> is pivotal in all UK legislation and
> is applied retrospectively to
> existing legislation."
>
> **REPLY:**
> "Oh gawd, more cross
> (angry) posting.
> Fuck the UN, fuck the
> galactic human rights
> commission. They are all
> part of the hegemonic
> conspectus and we
> survive without them not
> because of them.
> When you meet the man
> with the big stick do you
> quote law at him, or do
> you emulate Bruce Lee?"

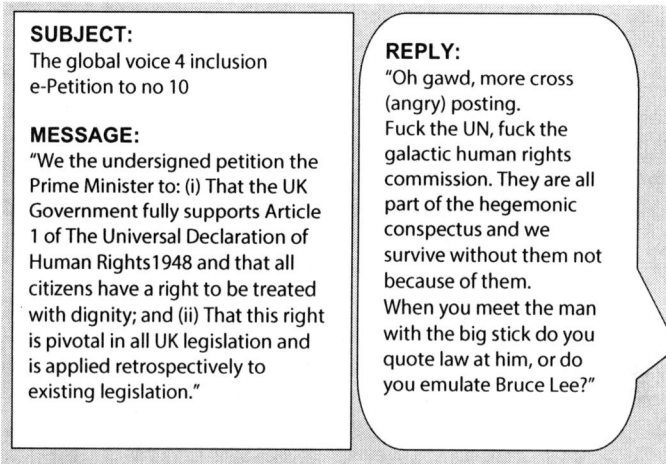

Figure 2.4. On hearing voices (e-mail exchange in response to Butler, March 31, 2010).

to create new data of such voices. Disabled people are, and have been, 'speaking for themselves' for years, but the necessary connections, and efforts to listen and seek out voices, have not always been made.

I wanted to find a rich diversity of the many competing, disagreeing, silent, messy, confused, out loud and proud, distant, hidden, organized and lost voices. I decided against 'representative' voices of the newly re-emerging, organized system of disability politics in Britain, which was caught up in structural limitations. I argued that it might distract me from thinking freely about future possibilities. Disability voices were taken from both published and unpublished material, as written voices and oral evidence, conversational interview data and research diaries, and observations and personal reflections. They were presented in multimodal fashion with the inclusion of and reference to a small number of photographic or pictorial representations, a DVD, poster campaigns and interactive internet resources designed by young disabled people, online access to video-clips, visual and sound files.

In no particular order, voices were collected from disabled academics to 'ordinary' disabled people of different ages and backgrounds, cultural practices, religious beliefs, gender and sexual orientation, and with different levels of political activism. They included individual disabled people and organizations of disabled people, disabled politicians, disabled teachers, trainee teachers, senior citizens, pupils and disabled young people. They included silent voices in the gaps of statistics. I noted under-represented voices in unfilled seats on management boards and in political office; refused voices in cinemas and on buses; and silenced voices outside polling stations. There were disturbing voices and alienated voices buried in legal case law narratives. Illustrative material from Germany and other international contexts complemented the picture at a European and more global level.

17

I wanted to pull out the 'inner essence' of disabled people's voices and run these over themes of citizenship, so that they were continually part of the zoom where the personal voices and political voices were mutually constitutive. The voices were provided by using evidence directly from disabled people (disabled voices) or disabled people's experiences (disability voices). This was achieved through the development and use of different forms of case analyses, such as embedded case study (Yin, 2003), case law analysis, and case scenarios, which were run over a multiplicity of situations and circumstances exemplifying or illuminating particular elements of citizenship. In that way I created mash-up methodology, thus creating a new sound of disability equality by use of empirically framed case analyses. I shall expand on the idea of creating a 'new song' in the subsequent paragraphs, which is then followed by examples of case study approach.

'Mash-up' is a Jamaican Creole term originally meaning 'to destroy', and in Hip Hop music this term refers to music made up entirely of different songs, different styles or genres usually considered to be incompatible. A 'Kylie Minogue versus New Order' or 'Chris Isaak versus Eminem' for instance, where one song's vocals run over the other's musical lines, resulting in, for example, 'Papa had a Rodeo'. Mash-up has been described as 'the highest form of musical re-contextualization' and 'pulls out the song's inner essence' (Cruger, 2006, online). A mash-up unsettles, is unexpected, implies no previous connection, at least to the minds of people who 'know' the dominant melody. They know it so well. People who are 'expert' in their traditional well rehearsed systems are invited to change *Denkmuster* to hear a new song.

A mash-up version seems wrong, awkward, challenging: almost threatening. It is in this unsettling, challenging edge that mash-up methodology is akin to applying critical theory. To the purist of tradition (in music as elsewhere) the mash-up version does not appear to fit together, such as hearing the distinct voice of Annie Lennox over a drum 'n' base musical line, or the ragged Eminem over loved Beatles melody. However, the present generation listens to the song as one creation, one entity, and one complete whole new sound. Mash-up implies something new has been created. In this way I sought to present a new song that respected disabled people.

Mash-up methodology produced a perspective with changed *Denkmuster* that was completed by the foregrounding of disability voices. I used a new set of vocabulary to express these ideas, for example, foregrounding happens when disability voices are run over a theme of citizenship. If, in citizenship education as elsewhere, we do not hear that voice on every page, then the complete 'whole' version of the song has been corrupted. In this vein, the 'rip-off' of which Oliver speaks in the opening quote is a form of corruption. To illustrate the corruption that occurs in traditional citizenship discussions which fail to run disabled voices over its themes, a brief example is offered.

In the introductory chapter of my thesis, I wrote about constitutions. I argued that despite different strands, citizenship was primarily a legal concept linked to a constitutional framework for nations. Constitutions contain the ground rules of government, they define how the state can exercise its power and the role of citizens in this regard, and they identify how money is to be raised and prioritised for spending. Constitutions elaborate on rules and principles of living together in a civic society and the nature of these rules change over time. This changing nature of constitutions can be exemplified by two examples, the first focuses on the Treaty Establishing the European Community – EEC Treaty (as amended) (European Union, 1957), and the second considers an Article in the German Basic Law (Grundgesetz der Bundesrepublic Deutschland – GG, 1994).

In 1957, the Treaty Establishing the European Community (European Union, 1957) not only created a trading community, but also established 'Citizenship of the Union' in Article 8 (1). The treaty proclaimed in Article 8 (2) that citizens 'shall enjoy the rights conferred by this treaty and shall be subject to the duties imposed thereof'. Disabled people are citizens. They have organized themselves to have a voice in Europe. The aim of the European Disability Forum (EDF) is 'to represent disabled people in dialogue with the European Union and other European authorities' and its mission is 'to promote equal opportunities for disabled people and to ensure disabled citizens' full access to fundamental and human rights through their active involvement in policy development and implementation in the European Union' (EDF, 2006, online). The president's address echoed UPIAS fundamental principles:

> Nothing about disabled people without disabled people is the motto of our movement, but also a basic principle of democracy. We will therefore continue to work at all levels to make sure that civil dialogue becomes a permanent reality in the region. It is a right we are asking for, not a favour. (Vardakastanis, 2006)

Basic human rights are enshrined as basic law within the first nineteen Articles of Germany's constitution (GG, 1994): 'The dignity of man shall be inviolable. To respect and protect it shall be the duty of state authority' (Article 1). To this extent, Article 3 deals with equality before the law: 'no-one may be disadvantaged or favoured because of his sex, his parentage, his race, his language, his homeland and origin, his faith, or his religious or political opinions'. With growing political pressure from disabled people, this provision was finally amended in 1994 to include disabled people in Article 3 (3): 'Niemand darf wegen seiner Behinderung benachteiligt werden' ('no-one must be disadvantaged on the basis of impairment/disability'). Article 3 (3) has been interpreted by disabled activists as meaning: 'Menschen mit Behinderungen ein Leben ohne Barrieren zu ermöglichen' ('to enable people with impairments a life without barriers') (Dahesh, 2000; 2004; Degener, 1995; Heiden, 1996; Hermes, 1994). Article 3 (3) is phrased in such a way as to allow for positive discrimination and more favourable treatment for disabled people in order to correct past injustices and remove barriers resulting there from.

Significantly, therefore, within mash-up methodology I needed to run disabled voices over the theme of constitutional legal rules. I could not talk about Article 8 of the European Convention on Human Rights (Council of Europe, 1950) without including the European Disability Forum in their own voice. I could not look at German non-discrimination clauses, Article 3 (3) of the German constitution, without citing disabled people whose political efforts had created and whose writings gave meaning to the otherwise abstract legal provision. The emerging picture was more than the two parts: constitutional legal rules on the one hand; and disabled people's responses or perspectives on the other. Instead, to run disabled voices over the theme of constitutional legal rules resulted in a fuller version of citizenship in the European Union, one that showed disabled people as constituting and actively engaging, first left out and later inserted in official text, as citizens struggling and campaigning in political discourse of the European Union.

A mash-up hears disabled voices not as additional ones to existing tunes, but as a constituent of a new and different song. Without this approach (running voices over themes), there is no 'pure' or neutral or objective approach to citizenship. Without it there is no 'professional' view of constitutional issues of the European Union, only a corrupted one. There is no 'European Union' without disabled people, there is no citizenship education without disability equality.

In my research, both quantitative and qualitative elements were used to frame and run disability voices over themes of citizenship. I applied three varieties of case study method in a 'teleological' sense, primarily to illuminate, to reveal not so much inadequacies, but a different picture. The aim was to connect disability equality to the concerns of educational practitioners in citizenship education. A dichotomy of quantitative and qualitative methods was not helpful as it failed to provide a meaningful distinction when finding out about disabled people's lived citizenship experiences.

For instance, in the case study 'AA Centrica' disabled people's action was embedded in a broader context of employment structures. Several stories were concurrently presented: disabled people's voices, disabled workers 'specially recruited', disabled employees later sacked, voices who were exercising political citizenship through protest and demonstrations, organised forms of disabled people's voices through the Disability Rights Commission and Trade Unions, as well as disabled people's action in taking recourse to the law. All of these different voices were run over the expanding and contracting economic pulse and context of the business (AA Centrica) over a period of several years. To complete the mash-up methodology the case analysis was further illuminated by reference to the voices of disabled academics in critical writings (for example, Abberley, 2002; Oliver, 1996; 2009; Oliver & Barnes, 1998).

Following Yin, the embedded case study is an empirical form of enquiry, where the goal is to describe the features, context, and process of a phenomenon (Yin, 2003). A critical analysis, however, and the rigorous application of the social model of disability, go beyond description and begin to make sense of facts, narratives and case presentations. In this way, material and discussions, like the AA Centrica case study, hears a polyphony of disability voices. I argued that mash-up material as in AA Centrica, will teach citizenship learners a way of thinking about how the law functions, about economic exigencies, about the opening up or closing down of opportunities and about the impact both law and economy has on the active citizenship of disabled people in different social situations. Without disability voices citizenship teaching in economics, law and social order is corrupt. For example, in 2002 citizenship became a statutory subject in England for 11 to 16 year-olds and part of a non-statutory framework at primary school (from age 5), yet five years later *Developing citizens* whilst claiming to provide 'an authoritative collection of key papers' (Breslin & Dufour, 2007, back cover) failed to include disability equality.

I sketched many disability voices over a particular citizenship theme, such as the theme of 'economic participation', 'political engagement', 'autonomy and choice', 'democratic participation' and 'identity and belonging'. During the collection of data, I was unclear about the overall shape of the PhD. It was an organic, accidental process that came together during the writing-up phase. The totality of single and embedded case studies, together with voices of disabled people from a very broad range of empirical sources performed the function of triangulation and thus increased the validity of the study. This richness provided persuasive evidence of both the need for and a method of connecting disability equality to citizenship education. The main activity was 'ideological critical thinking' within the personal – political zoom of active involvement of disabled people. As Oliver observed, 'to say that I don't have an ideological position is in fact an ideological position. It's bizarre that most people don't recognize that' (quoted from an interview by Allan & Slee, 2008, p. 58).

Significant impact of my research findings in the teaching and learning of citizenship in schools remains illusionary. When the 'citizenship, diversity and identity' strand was reviewed in the National Curriculum, disability was again left out. I fear that these gaps cannot be filled simply by having a 'disability and citizenship' pack on the shelves at school or by running 'disability awareness' sessions, because whilst resources have been developed with and by disabled people, they are not always consistently framed within the social model. Significantly, even if they were so intentioned, they failed to penetrate the core of professional practice or institutional arrangements. For instance, the extent to which a teacher is or is not grounded in the social model of disability, becomes an important determinant for the way children's imagination can be recruited and their understanding and emancipation on disability equality enhanced. The question is not so much whether a teacher is disabled, given the low numbers who disclose an impairment or health condition, but which perspective or understanding that teacher brings with them, the level of their 'emancipated' self.

INSIGHTS ABOUT MY RESEARCH GAINED AS A RESULT OF WRITING THIS CHAPTER

Authenticity is the challenge for disability research and to address this I developed a mash-up methodology with three key elements: transformative agenda, relevance to the lived experiences of disabled people and significant impact. The application of running polyphonic disability voices over controversial themes tells us more about the structural forces in society than any one of these voices could do by themselves. In combination this mash-up offered a rich tapestry of authenticity, which empirically drew together a wide range of data sources and provided a context for patterns of thinking about citizenship issues.

On reflection, I regret that at an institutional level the final element remained largely illusionary. Stubborn structural forces counteracted significant progress and, in fact, there were signs of regression: in other words things were getting worse for disabled people. Yet, I experienced, how liberating research and the imagination of future possibilities, had the potential to empower disabled people (people with impairments or with long-term health conditions).

Disabled people did not agree with each other and there was a mash-up of voices. Running over the political citizenship themes were disabled voices involved in, or promoting, a broad spectrum of political campaigning methods, whether close to or away from government: protests, political lobbying, education and persuasion, poster campaigns, democratic participation, voting behaviour, self-organisation, internationalism, recourse to the law, direct action and civil disobedience. Others were simply keeping their heads down. I concluded that there was no 'one' voice or 'true' voice or 'objective' voice. In the same way as dissonance, a note or chord outside the prevailing harmony, was vital in understanding the overall tonal and harmonic quality of music *Klangqualität*. Apparently conflicting or contradictory voices were necessary in completing the mash-up of voices over a theme of citizenship.

The cartoon by my father symbolizes various successful dissemination approaches. I used *Justicia* to support human rights training as well as presentations given to research students on the personal – political zoom in disability equality research (Reichart, 2009; 2010). I gave permission for *Justicia* to feature in training material developed and disseminated with, for and by disabled people, such as on the front cover of *Disability is a human rights issue: A guide to human rights for disabled people* (Leicestershire Centre for Integrated Living, 2010). The cartoon also greeted visitors to the Disability Awareness in Action (DAA) internet page on justice, whilst I was researching and editing for this international network on disability human rights stories across the globe. In other words, key outcomes of my research *Connecting disability equality to citizenship education* (Reichart, 2007), resulted in my own re-positioning: moving closer to grass-roots activism and further away from academia, of writing simultaneously from 'with-out' academic institutions, whilst not aligning myself to 'within' a particular disability organization.

Dissemination continues to remain a challenge. Widening the 'emancipated knowledge' reach, in particular on human rights and the role of law, is envisaged through disability politics, information networks and disabled people's organizations but largely 'out-with' academic institutions. There is a weaker dissemination, that keeps me earning a living: *Justicia* with a mash-up of disability voices is used as a methodology in training sessions and presentations to health and social welfare professionals, housing experts, board of directors of public or private services, government departments, and leaders in the education sector. In this way, stubborn institutional barriers continue to be challenged.

A FINAL WORD

This timely reflection has reminded me of the power of direct experiences with 'out and proud' disabled people. It has warned me of the potential of being crushed under the weight of existing structures and power relations. We need to join together in solidarity and action to create a 'new song'. For people with and without impairments or long term health conditions, thinking is a necessary but not sufficient element in our liberation.

Unfinished Business: What is left to do, other than to start again at the beginning?

To engage the **personal – political zoom** in a way that both respects diverse personal narratives of impairment or long-term health conditions and asks critical questions of the law, within its socio-legal context, as it continues to fail disabled women.

To apply the **mash-up methodology** to constellations of power in our 'throwaway' consumer society, so that disabled and disability voices energize transformative knowledge, in order to challenge the effects of the expanding and contracting pulses of recession.

REFERENCES

Abberley, P. (1995). Disabling ideology in health and welfare – the case of occupational therapy. *Disability & Society, 10*(2), 221–232.

Abberley, P. (2002). Work, disability, disabled people and European social theory. In C. Barnes, M. Oliver & L. Barton (Eds.), *Disability studies today* (pp. 120–138). Cambridge: Polity/Blackwell Publisher.

Adept (2004). *Behaviour change model.* Disability equality training material. Retrieved May 3, 2012, from http://www.adept-uk.org/Training/

Allan, J., & Slee, R. (2008). *Doing inclusive education research.* Rotterdam: Sense Publishers.

Barnes, C. (1991). *Disabled people in Britain and discrimination: A case for anti-discrimination legislation.* London: Hurst & Co.

Barnes, C., & Mercer, G. (2010). *Exploring disability.* Cambridge: Polity.

Barton, L. (Ed.). (1997). *The politics of special educational needs.* Lewes: Falmer Press.

Barton, L. (2005). Emancipatory research and disabled people: Some observations. *Educational Review, 57*(3), 317–327.

Barton, L., & Oliver, M. (Eds.). (1997). *Disability studies: Past, present and future.* Leeds: Disability Press.

Breslin, T., & Dufour, B. (2007). *Developing citizens: A comprehensive introduction to effective citizenship education in the secondary school.* London: Hodder Murray.

Butler, S. (2010). *E-petition 'Dignity for all'.* Retrieved June 5, 2010, from hhtp://petitions.number10. gov/dignityforall/

Case of Kutzner v Germany (2002). *Judgment of February 26, 2002,* REF00003286. Retrieved May 3, 2012, from http://www.nkmr.org/english/kutzner_v_germany.htm

Council of Europe. (1950). *European convention on human rights, Article 8*. Retrieved May 3, 2012, from http://www.hri.org/docs/ECHR50.html

Cruger, R. (2006). *The mash-up revolution*. Retrieved May 3, 2012, from http://remixtheory.net/?p=19

Dahesh, K. (2000). In Deutschland ist e simmer noch nicht normal verschieden zu sein. Zur Situation von Menschen mit Behinderungen. [In Germany it is still not normal to be different. On the situation of disabled people]. *Frankfurter Rundschau*, November 29.

Dahesh, K. (2004). *Ein Rückfall in die Gesellschaftliche Isolation droht: Zehn Jahre nach Verankerung des Benachteiligungsverbots für behinderte Menschen im Grundgesetz macht der Rotstift Erfolge zunichte.* [Danger of regression into social isolation: Ten years on, red tape is ruining any progress on non-discrimination enshrined as human rights for disabled people]. *Frankfurter Rundschau*, December 31.

Degener, T. (1995). Disabled persons and human rights: The legal framework. In T. Degener & Y. Koster (Eds.), *Human rights and disabled people: Essays and relevant human rights instruments* (pp. 9–39). Dortrecht: Martinus Nijhoff.

Department for Work and Pensions (DWP). (2005). *The Disability Discrimination Act*. London: HMSO.

Department for Work and Pensions (DWP). (2010). *The Equality Act*. London: HMSO.

Disability News Service, (2011). *Government sparks anger after weakening Equality Act duties*. Retrieved May 3, 2012, from http://www.disabilitynewsservice.com/index.php/2011/03/ government-sparks-anger-after-weakening-equality-act-duties/

Eagleton, T. (1994). Ideology and its vicissitudes in Western Marxism. In S. Zizek (Ed.), *Mapping ideology*. London: Verso.

European Union. (1957). *Treaty establishing the European Community (as amended by subsequent treaties)*. Retrieved July 3, 2012, from http://www.hri.org/docs/Rome57/Part2.html

European Disability Forum (EDF). (2006). *Welcome message*. Retrieved April 5, 2006, from http://www.edf-feph.org/

Forum Behinderter Juristinnen und Juristen. (1995). *Vorschläge für Gleich-stellungsvorschriften, Kap.3: Rechte behinderter Frauen im Arbeitsleben und in der Rehabilitation, und Kap.5b zum Betreuungsgesetz [Recommendations for specific legal regulation on equalization, chapter 3: Legal rights of disabled women in employment and in rehabilitation programs, and chapter 5b in relation to the law on support, care and assistance]*. Kassel: ISL.

Gooding, C. (2010a). *Speaking against proposed changes in application of specific duties under the Equality Act 2010* (RADAR debate). Retrieved December 2, 2010, from www.radar.org.uk/wp.../05/RADAR-2010-Debate-ms-011110.doc

Gooding, C. (2010b). *Don't wreck duty!* Retrieved December 2, 2010, from http://www.radar.org.uk

Grundgesetz der Bundesrepublic Deutschland (GG) (1994). *in der Fassung vom November 15, 1994 ; Art. 3, Abs. 3, Satz 2 : Niemand darf wegen seiner Behinderung benachteiligt werden. [Basic law and fundamental rights in Federal Republic of Germany constitution, version of November 15, 1994, article 3(3), no one shall be discriminated against because of disability]*. Retrieved July 3, 2012, from http://www.gesetze-im-internet.de/bundesrecht/gg/gesamt.pdf

Habermas, J. (1987). Theorie des kommunikativen Handelns (McCarthy, Trans.). *The theory of communicative action: Volume 2, lifeworld and system, a critique of functionalist reason*. Cambridge: Polity.

Habermas, J. (1992). *Between facts and norms: Contributions to a discourse theory of law and democracy* (Studies in contemporary German social thought). Massachusetts: MIT Press.

Hatch, J. A. (2002). *Doing qualitative research in education settings*. Albany NY: State University of New York Press.

Heiden, H. (1996). Niemand darf wegen seiner Behinderung benachteiligt warden [Nobody should be discriminated against because of disability]. *Grundrecht und Alltag – eine Bestandsaufnahme*. Hamburg: RoRoRo Verlag.

Held, D. (1992). *Introduction to critical theory: Horkheimer to Habermas*. Calofornia: University of California Press.

Hendriks, A., & Degener, T. (1994). The evolution of a European perspective on disability legislation. *European Journal of Health Law, 1*(4), 343–363.

Hermes, G. (1994). *Mit Recht verschieden sein: Forderungen behinderter Frauen an Gleichstellungsgesetze, Schriftreihe zum selbstbestimmten Leben Behinderter. [To be rightfully different: Disabled women's demands for anti-discrimination law].* Kassel: bifos-Schriftenreihe.

Hermes, G. (1998). *Krücken, babys und barrieren – Zur situation behinderter Eltern in der Bundesrepublik [Crutches, babies and barriers – On the situation of disabled parents in the Federal Republic of Germany].* Kassel: bifos-Schriftenreihe.

Hermes, G. (2002). *Tabu? Elternschaft körper und sinnesbehinderter menschen, zusammen 6/02, S. 4–7, [Still a taboo? Active parenthood and people with physical or sensory impairments, together].* Kassel: bifos-Schriftenreihe.

Hermes, G. (2004). *Behinderung und elternschaft leben: Kein Widerspruch, Eine Studie zum Unterstützungsbedarf körper und sinnesbehinderter Eltern in Deutschland [Disability and parenthood: No contradiction. A study on the support requirements of parents with physical or sensory impairments in Germany.* AG Spak Bücher, Neu-Ulm.

Kellner, D. (2003). Toward a critical theory of education. *Democracy & Nature, 9*(1), 51–64.

Leicestershire Centre for Integrated Living (LCIL). (2010). *Disability is a human rights issue: A guide to human rights for disabled people* (original cartoon by disabled activist Joe Reichart). Leicester: LCIL.

Morris, J. (2005). *Citizenship and disabled people.* London: Disability Rights Commission.

Oliver, M. (1990). *The politics of disablement.* Basingstoke: Macmillan.

Oliver, M. (1996). *Understanding disability: From theory to practice.* London: Macmillan.

Oliver, M. (1997). Emancipatory research: Realistic goal or impossible dream? In C. Barnes & G. Mercer (Eds.), *Doing disability research* (pp. 15–31). Leeds: The Disability Press.

Oliver, M. (2009). (2nd ed.) *Understanding disability: From theory to practice.* Basingstoke: Palgrave Macmillan.

Oliver, M., & Barnes, C. (1998). *Social policy and disabled people: From exclusion to inclusion.* London: Longman.

Oliver, M., & Barnes, C. (2012). *The new politics of disablement.* Basingstoke: Palgrave Macmillan.

Oliver, M., & Barton, L. (2000). *The emerging field of disability studies: A view from Britain.* Retrieved May 3, 2012, from http://www.leeds.ac.uk/disability-studies/archiveuk/Oliver/Emerging%20field.pdf

Reichart, M. (2007). *Connecting disability equality to citizenship education.* PhD thesis. University of Greenwich.

Reichart, M. (2009). Researching disability equality: The personal and the political. *Keynote presentation at EdD weekend, University of Greenwich, UK,* November 20–22.

Reichart, M. (2010). Stubborn structural forces and signs of regression: How things are getting worse for disabled people. *Paper presented at the University of London, UK,* November 24.

Scott, D., & Usher, R. (1999). *Researching education.* London: Cassell.

Slee, R. (2001). Social justice and the changing directions in educational research: The case of inclusive education. *International Journal of Inclusive Education, 5*(2–3), 167–177.

Union of the Physically Impaired Against Segregation (UPIAS). (1975). *Fundamental principles of disability.* Retrieved May 3, 2012, from http://www.leeds.ac.uk/disability-studies/archiveuk/UPIAS/fundamental%20principles.pdf

United Nations. (2006). *Convention on the rights of persons with disabilities.* Retrieved on August 28, 2013, from: http://www.un.org/esa/socdev/enable/documents/tccconve.pdf

Vardakastanis, Y. (2006). European models of funding of disabled people organizations. *Paper presented at the Balkan Regional Conference,* March 19. Retrieved December 5, 2006, from http://www.edf-feph.org/Page_Generale.asp?DocID=13874&thebloc=13885

Yin, R. K. (2003). *Case study research* (3rd ed.). London: Sage.

Young, M. (2007). Durkheim and Vygotsky's theories of knowledge and the implication for a critical education theory. *Critical Studies in Education, 48*(1), 43–62.

CARMEL KELLY

3. RESEARCHING DISABILITY DISCOURSES, USER CONSTRUCTS AND PRACTITIONER PERSPECTIVES IN CARE MANAGEMENT PRACTICES

INTRODUCTION

The social model of disability has been of critical significance in naming disability as a form of social oppression, in challenging discriminatory practices, championing agendas for inclusion and privileging modes of enquiry that facilitate the achievement of those aims. One measure of its influence is the apparent insertion and validation of social model ideas in political, policy, academic and practitioner discourses. However, some of the fault lines and contradictions attendant on such seemingly seismic discursive shifts are reflected in Oliver's (2004) observations that while many may claim to be social modellists, the social model appears to have had no significant impact on professional practice.

It is this question of the disconnection between the official privileging of social model principles and their perceived negligible influence on practice that my research sought to address. Thus, the research project, undertaken as part of a PhD program was an attempt to explore, in a particular welfare setting, whether and what influence the social model had on everyday practices. In this chapter, I firstly, outline the main features and key objectives of the research project. Secondly, I discuss why I chose this particular research topic and why I adopted an ethnographic methodology. Thirdly, I consider a range of research problems and ethical dilemmas I experienced and the power relationships that those dilemmas signify. In this context, I also indicate strategies that facilitated the production of a more balanced and considered research account. Fourthly, I outline key research findings and discuss the usefulness of the research particularly in relation to emancipatory imperatives. In the concluding section, I discuss problematic and positive aspects of the research and consider how some emergent themes might be further developed.

MY RESEARCH PROJECT

The research setting was a local authority care management team whose duties included the assessment, monitoring and review of physically disabled people's eligibility for adult social care services. Significantly, according to official council policy, service provision was informed by social model principles. The choice of research design was a case study and its centerpiece was a year-long period of observation. The

S. Symeonidou and K. Beauchamp-Pryor (Eds.), Purpose, Process and Future Direction of Disability Research, 27–43.

research role I adopted was one of 'peripheral membership' (Adler & Adler, 1994) in which I observed and interacted closely with team members without adopting a practitioner role. Other research methods included semi-structured interviews with team members and analysis of relevant documents.

The research questions as broadly formulated were:

– What are the dominant disability and user discourses in care management practices?
– What is the position of social model or user-centered discourses in this context?
– How are practitioners positioned and how do they position themselves in relation to those disability and user discourses?
– What are the mechanisms through which user needs are assessed and determined?
– What appear to be the most important factors that shape and inform decision-making?
– Are care management practices and processes disciplinary in effect?

The purpose of these questions was to develop an understanding not only of the dominant discourses, but also of the interplay of differentiated discursive practices, the consequent positioning of social model and user-centered discourses, and the disciplinary matrix through which care management practices were produced. More specifically, the research aims were to gain insights into practitioner ideas, beliefs and attitudes towards disability, disabled people, social services users and particularly the disabled users who were the subjects/objects of their intervention. I also hoped to clarify research participants' perceptions of their roles as practitioners and to explore some anticipated points of resonance and dissonance between official guidelines and front-line strategies.

There were a number of reasons why, from a social model perspective, these questions seemed important. Firstly, while disabled people have been the subjects/ objects of much mainstream social science research, less critical attention has been paid to those claiming expertise in the management of disabled people. Secondly, as direct assessors of user need, interpreters of official policies and distributors of resources, care managers and their supervisors occupy positions of relative power.

Therefore, their actions or inactions impact significantly on the material and social circumstances of the disabled people with whom they come in contact. Furthermore, the policy interpretations and decision-making processes in which practitioners are engaged are shaped by and, in turn, engender socially constructed understandings of what disability means, what it means to be disabled and what it means to be a service user. However, the personal significance I attach to such questions only makes sense in the context of broader influences that have shaped my concerns, motivations and interests. It is those formative influences I discuss in the next section.

FORMATIVE INFLUENCES ON CHOICE OF RESEARCH PROJECT

The choice and focus of the research project stemmed from a confluence of work experience, personal history, political orientation and engagement with a range of sociological, social policy and social work texts. Prior to detailing such influences, it seems important to clarify why I consider such disclosure to be appropriate. The rationale, both currently and at the time of constructing the research account, for sharing with the reader some of my key research related ideas, interests, beliefs, values and experiences stem from my perspective that one's ideology or world view shape both what is sought and what is found in the research process (Bines, 1995; Vernon, 1997). By making my position as a researcher more visible I, therefore, eschew any claims to the objectivity or definitive 'truth' of the research account but, hopefully, also facilitate a more informed, engaged and critical reading of the research itself.

Ideological Standpoint

The baggage I brought to the research project was, firstly, a political critique of the role of welfare agencies in sustaining rather than challenging an iniquitous status quo. Secondly, while opposed to the privatizing, market oriented, managerialist and budgetary imperatives of the neo-liberal agenda (Langan, 1998; Newman, 1998), I considered the 'old' bureau professional welfare regimes (Clarke, 1998) and the unequal practitioner/user power relationships produced therein as equally problematic. In the latter context, my prior work experience as a local authority social worker created an awareness of the gulf between acclaimed professional values of respect for persons (Timms, 1964) and front-line cultures that engendered negative 'labeling' of social service users' actions and behaviors (Satyamurti, 1981; Simpkin, 1979).

My ideological standpoint was also informed by a feminist perspective that focused on the patriarchal underpinnings of the welfare state (Dominelli & McLeod, 1989; Wilson, 1977) and the specific forms of oppression experienced by women both as social services users and employees (Hallett, 1989; Healy, 2005). Nonetheless, however flawed the state social work/social care enterprise might be, I considered there was still value in its commitment to concepts of human solidarity, its attempted engagement with those who are poorly served by hegemonic social structures (Bailey & Brake, 1975) and its implicit rejection of dominant social norms of individualism, competition, and material success. With regard to social work in particular and welfare practices in general, my pre-research position could therefore be summarized as critical, reflective, ambivalent and uncertain.

Personal History and Social Model Awareness

Another influence on my choice of research topic was my experience of chronic illness that brought my welfare career to a premature close but also introduced me to the social model of disability. I became ill with myalgic encephalomyelitis, which at the time of onset of my illness was, and to a lesser extent still is, a highly contested category of impairment. However, engagement with social model ideas

(Morris, 1991; Oliver, 1990; Oliver & Barnes, 2012) enabled me to understand the socially created oppressive character of my 'invalid' status and the possibility and potential of resistance. Moreover, social model ideas were particularly pertinent to developing my thinking on welfare practices. In this context, social model critiques of the historically significant role of welfare practitioners in constructing and sustaining deficit models of disability (Barnes, 1990; Barton, 1989; Priestley, 1999) both echoed and heightened my own concerns. In a more immediate sense, the spark that ignited my research interest was a discussion I had with a group of social work students who were 'doing' the social model as part of their qualifying course. In reply to my question of how the social model might be applied to their own practice, one student suggested that when they were at work they just did as they were told. The inference appeared to be that similar strategies applied to their work as students. It was this expression of the need and ability to produce dominant institutional norms, however contradictory, depending on one's specific role context that helped to crystallize, for me, a central theme of the research.

Foucauldian Influences on the Theoretical Framework

In attempting to construct a theoretical framework within which such questions might be addressed, I was greatly influenced by Foucauldian ideas and constructs. In a general sense, one of the appeals of a Foucauldian position was its invitation to question the self-evident, to challenge the familiar, to re-examine institutions (Foucault, 1988), to critically consider their necessity and to privilege concepts of contingency rather than inevitability in their formation. Of more particular interest to the research project were the privileging in Foucauldian discourses of power and power relationships (Foucault, 1982), the emphases on the interconnectedness of knowledge, power and discourse formation (Foucault, 1980) and the deconstruction of power in terms of disciplinary and pastoral modalities (Foucault, 1991a).

Furthermore, Foucault's attention to the body as a locus upon and through which power relations were produced (Foucault, 1991b), the construction of the examination as a normalizing mechanism and the exposition of panoptic modes of surveillance (Foucault, 1991a) seemed to offer a challenging and radical perspective from which to critically examine dominant discourses and disciplinary practices in care management. Finally, a Foucauldian analysis of liberation practices as not necessarily ending repression, but rather producing a new set of power relations and discursive practices (Foucault & Deleuze, 1977) seemed to me to both highlight the need for and facilitate critical analysis of radical discourses such as the social model. The theoretical underpinning of the research and the development of my research standpoint were therefore informed by both social model and Foucauldian insights.

A further key element in the construction of the research project was the adoption of an ethnographic methodology. In the next section, I indicate why an ethnographic approach seemed the most appropriate.

REASONS FOR CHOOSING A PARTICULAR RESEARCH
METHODOLOGY AND METHODS

I chose an ethnographic orientation for a number of reasons. Firstly, the ethnographic focus on micro-practices (Silverman, 2000) reflected my own desire to find out what was 'really' happening at the 'coalface' of practice. Secondly, an ethnographic position reinforced my ideological orientation that the biography/standpoint of the observer may shape what is observed and recorded (Sapsford & Abbott, 1992) and that power relationships are critically significant in the construction of research (Allan, 1999). Finally, the appropriateness of this methodology was indicated by the privileging in ethnographic discourses of the contextual, emergent aspects of cultural forms (Clifford, 1986), the adoption of an open-minded approach (Davis, 2006) and the development of reflexive practices (Hey, 1997). While acknowledging tensions and contradictions within and between these discourses, I considered that the juxtaposition of social model, Foucauldian and ethnographic perspectives encouraged an interrogative and reflexive research approach that facilitated engagement with the complex, the paradoxical and the unexpected in the study of everyday practices.

Of more immediate relevance to my particular research project was the fact that an ethnographic approach, with its emphasis on prolonged periods of observation, was compatible with my objective to develop a deeper understanding of the formal and informal processes that shape practices. An ethnographic orientation also facilitated the deployment of a variety of data sources (Yin, 1994). Thus a combination of observational and interviewing strategies would, I hoped, help clarify points of convergence and divergence between practitioners' representation of practice and material practices whilst documentary analysis would enhance understanding of the institutional contexts within which everyday practices were produced (Strauss & Corbin, 1990). Therefore, the justification for the combination of observational, interviewing and documentary material was that it would help to illuminate some of the tensions and ambiguities of care management practices that either data collection strategy alone would not achieve. While the effectiveness of this approach is discussed later in the chapter, it seems important to acknowledge that the research project was not simply constituted through the individual influences and intellectual rationalizations already outlined. Of equal significance were my attitudes towards the research, which I indicate in the next section.

Attitudes Towards the Research Project

My excitement at the prospect of doing this research was fuelled by my curiosity to identify factors which had changed or remained familiar, since I had worked in social services departments many years previously. However, I was also anxious because of my relative lack of experience and knowledge of research, and my ability to meet the academic demands of the PhD course. Such anxieties were tempered by supportive supervision, previous occupational and academic experiences and a degree of confidence that my insider/outsider status as a social worker/researcher in a care management team positioned me well to reflect and comment on the practices I would observe.

From the outset, I felt that as a self-funding student in an educational rather than a social work environment, I enjoyed a considerable amount of autonomy and freedom to pursue the research in ways that seemed fruitful to me. As the research progressed, I became even more aware of the advantages of this position although, of course, a corollary of this was a sense of isolation and disconnection.

I have no doubt that it was my absorption in the subject, my perception of the relevance and to some degree the originality of the findings, coupled with the time/commitment expended, that enabled me to complete the project despite the difficulties encountered. In the next section, I discuss some of these difficulties.

RESEARCH PROBLEMS AND DILEMMAS

Skeggs (2001) refers to 'irreconcilable conflicts' as a feature of ethnographic research. The primary conflicts I perceived were between the practical imperatives to ensure that access to the research site was gained and maintained, ethnographic imperatives to adopt non-judgmental approaches and open-ended strategies and ethical imperatives to ensure that participants had sufficient knowledge about research processes and purposes to give informed consent. In the following sections, I discuss these conflicts and difficulties and strategies deployed to manage them.

Finding a Sample

The most significant obstacle to commencing the research was to find a team that was willing to consider my presence as a researcher. In the end, a chance remark made in the course of a telephone conversation with an ex-social work manager led me to the manager of the team in which the research took place. Following protracted delays partly to do with departmental reorganization but also involving delicate negotiations regarding not only the researcher's role but also the responsibilities of the academic supervisor, permission was finally granted for research to commence. Almost a year had elapsed from the time the initial approach had been made. Thus, with hindsight, successful access was gained through a combination of chance, coincidence and perseverance.

Presenting the Researcher/Research

Access difficulties also highlighted the critical importance of researcher/research presentation (Burgess, 1987; Johnson, 1975). To maximize the possibility of success, I therefore adopted a number of strategies. Firstly, I stressed the consensual character of research participants' involvement. Secondly, in constructing what I considered would be an acceptable researcher persona, I drew attention to my partial insider status as a professionally qualified social worker in order to indicate my potential for empathy and understanding of practice. In similar vein, I was open with team members about being chronically ill, not least because of the limitations it might impose on research but I affected silence on the politicizing effects of the illness. Thirdly, research aims and questions were phrased in generalist and neutral tones. For example, one of the stated aims was to examine how the experiences of disability and disabled people are perceived within the context of practice but no specific mention was made of the social model of disability.

Ethical Dilemmas Related to Partial Disclosure of Research Aims and Purposes

The discussion on access and presentation illustrates my attempts to resolve difficulties through the adoption of a number of obfuscatory strategies. I now consider such strategies both in terms of how I justified them and the ethical issues they raised. Had I been totally open regarding my social modellist position, I think it unlikely that access would have been granted. I was acutely aware that, as Swain (1995) suggests, research that is perceived as overtly challenging is not likely to be permitted. Furthermore, the development of positive relationships with practitioners in the field would, in my judgment, have been potentially seriously compromised had I explicitly presented myself as a social modellist. More specifically, since officially, everyday practices were supposed to be guided by social model principles, the presence of a researcher claiming allegiance to such principles would most probably have been perceived as a threat. The likely consequences of this would have been that research participants would be even less willing to engage with me, and would be likely to adopt defensive positions thus producing a highly circumscribed range of responses. Bines (1995) and Allan and Slee (2008) use similar rationales for nondisclosure of researcher positions.

However, such practices of partial or nondisclosure seem to sail perilously close to positivistic constructions of the observer as detached and neutral or perhaps even more ambiguously of the ideal researcher simulating a position of neutrality in order to get a research 'result'. Thus, it may be that, as Murphy and Dingwall (2001) suggest, all research is located on a continuum between overtness and covertness. Nonetheless, however finely balanced judgments on partial disclosure and rationalizations of presentation may be, it seems inescapable that they are not morally neutral. Thus, although I did share as much information with research participants as seemed feasible and sensible, I am still uneasy about the partial character of that information. Another troubling aspect of the research role I adopted was the perceived need to maintain a non-judgmental mask, to feign disinterest in and to leave unchallenged practices and views I found disturbing. While such a passive stance may be deemed to be appropriate and even necessary from an ethnographic perspective, it seems highly problematic from a social model position. Finally, I think it is questionable how effective research strategies of partial disclosure are. My 'hunch' would be that I was seen as a social model person anyway.

This discussion illustrates the extent to which apparently clear and incontestable ethical and research norms such as a commitment to transparency, accuracy and best practice may in the construction of the research process become more opaque, ambiguous, conflicted and problematic. In such fraught and slippery terrain, the strategies through which I tried, however imperfectly, to maintain an ethical stance were to recognize and reflect on the dilemmas as they unfolded and to make decisions in the context of the commitments given to participants with regard to consent, confidentiality, and overall safeguarding of their interests.

Counter-strategies of Nondisclosure Amongst Research Participants

However, strategies of obfuscation and nondisclosure are not the sole prerogative of the researcher. As Cohen and Manion (1989) suggest, all parties to the research process may engage in withholding strategies. Thus, with regard to the research project, the formal responsibilities of team members were to allow me reasonable access to individual and team activities. However, in effect, they were the gatekeepers who determined what constituted reasonable access. Thus, certain activities such as attendance at team meetings, training days, gaining access to relevant documents and permission to interview all team members seemed unproblematic. However, attempts to enter the inner sanctum of the care management 'confessional' in order to observe core tasks such as user/care manager interviews or supervision sessions had very mixed success. Individual practitioners to varying degrees used a number of strategies ranging from controlled facilitation to resistance to outright refusal to ensure that what I observed of their 'private' transactions with users and supervisors was largely what they allowed me to see.

Thus, the formal contract suggested the location of the research in dominant social relations of research production where the researcher largely establishes the agenda, topics and tone of the research and the researched provide the research material. However, my de facto dependence on the co-operation and goodwill of research participants indicates some of the complexities of power relationships produced in the research setting. I consider these in more detail in the next section.

POWER RELATIONSHIPS

In terms of power relationships I, firstly, draw attention to the perceived vulnerability and anxieties of all those engaged in the research process. Secondly, I discuss the impact of gender on the construction of relationships in the field. Finally, I consider some positive outcomes and unresolved issues in the fraught arena of researcher/ researched relationships.

Vulnerability and Anxieties in the Research Setting

My ongoing sense of powerlessness and vulnerability was grounded in an anxiety that the research would not proceed, or that having commenced, it might be terminated at any time and that some or all of the research participants would not co-operate. Occasional comments such as one suggestion that it would be better if I went to other agencies fuelled this sense of anxiety. In the field notes, there were at least ten references to my concern that I might lose my desk. Clearly, for me, 'losing' my desk was highly symbolic of 'losing' the research. From the perspective of team members, I sensed that their sense of powerlessness stemmed from the destabilizing and alienating effects of being observed, recorded and written 'about' in a perhaps threatening and to some extent feared academic discourse, over which they would have no control. There seemed to be an all-pervasive concern that I would judge them negatively. There also appeared to be an anxiety that I was a management 'plant'. This was expressed most dramatically in a direct question I was asked as to whether I was a 'spy'.

Gender Issues

Given the complex intersections of power relationships and gender, it seems important to consider whether and in what ways, research processes and outcomes were influenced by my presence as a female researcher in a team where male and female members were evenly balanced. While it is not possible to reach any definitive conclusions, I believe that this particular gender mix was of some significance with regard to access issues, relationships with research participants and research activities.

Initial feedback from team members suggested that I was acceptable to team members because I was perceived as 'sensitive', someone who would not be 'pushy' and who was not a 'highflying professor'. Such ascribed characteristics suggest that, from the perspective of participants, I conformed to the stereotypical image of a non-threatening female researcher (Warren, 1988). This positioning, in turn, may have mitigated anxieties about my status and power and facilitated ongoing access to and engagement with team members. In terms of engagement, however, I felt that female team members were on the whole much more willing than their male counterparts to accede to my request to observe their interventions with users even though, as already suggested, the specific sites of observation were always determined by them. It may be that the more co-operative attitudes of female participants reflected their gendered positioning as more concerned with the needs and feelings of others (Cameron, 2002). It is also possible that female team members were more co-operative because they felt more of a sense of gender identification with me as indeed I did with them, although I recognize the importance of not confusing ease of communication with gender identification (Phoenix, 1994). Conversely, it is possible that male participants were more confident about and effective at resisting pressure for researcher involvement. This was evidenced by one male team member who claimed work pressure as a reason for not involving me but later laughed about the fact that he had been 'very uncooperative'.

There was also evidence of differentiated, gendered perceptions as to what constituted an appropriate researcher role. Given that some users were constructed as difficult, potentially violent and home visits consequently challenging, I offered to accompany team members on such visits simply on the grounds that an additional person might offer some degree of support or protection. While such offers were, on occasions, accepted by female team members, male members declined to take up my invitation. Such behavior may reflect dominant gendered social norms that render it more acceptable for women than men to acknowledge their vulnerability in situations deemed to be potentially dangerous (Entwistle, 1998). By contrast, some male team members invited me to be a note-taker at multidisciplinary meetings. My informal status, in this context, as quasi-administrative/personal assistant, while ideally suited to my observer role, suggests that female researchers may be assigned to traditionally subordinated gender roles in a field setting.

However, it seems important not to overstate the significance of gender effects in the construction of my research relationships. Thus, for instance, one of the most enthusiastic supporters of the research was a male team manager. Furthermore, the most significant factors in sustaining the project were positive personal interactions with all research participants and a sense of reciprocity engendered by telling jokes, stories, sharing aspects of life histories and the common experience of being, however tangentially for me, a part of the team over a period of a year.

Partial Resolution of and Unresolved Tensions in Researcher/Researched Relationships

The relative success of mutual strategies of negotiation and accommodation is indicated in the results of a questionnaire completed at the end of the field research. Those who responded expressed overall satisfaction with the research experience and stated that they would regard the prospect of granting access to another researcher very positively. However, the sense of exclusion and relative powerlessness some participants may have felt is reflected in one comment that team members should have been more involved in the actual research process in terms of data collection and interpretation. I consider that such a degree of involvement would not have been appropriate. Nonetheless, I regret that, in the post-observation period, I did not discuss the research findings in more detail with research participants. However, my decision to evade potentially hostile reaction to my findings indicates the relatively more powerful position of the researcher as he/she leaves the field and focuses on the construction of a research account.

It is in the context of the research problems and dilemmas as outlined, that I now consider the appropriateness of my choice of research methodology.

APPROPRIATENESS OF RESEARCH METHODOLOGY

In reflecting on this question, I consider how each of the three research methods of the case study (observation, interviews and documentary analysis), both separately and in combination, served my research purposes.

Firstly, the observation process was of central significance in the identification, elucidation and formation of the central themes of the research story. It offered insights into the 'inner workings' of the organization, how decisions were made, the factors that appeared to shape decision-making and perhaps most importantly an all-pervasive if 'hidden' care management 'canteen culture' that engendered defensive practitioner and negative user positions. The observation data also influenced the form and content of interview questions and, in my opinion, provided a sense of immediacy and relevance to the concerns of interviewees.

Secondly, the interview setting offered a space where I could explore with each research participant in privacy and some depth, questions relevant to the research. In addition, it offered an opportunity to redress what I felt was the sometimes uneven, haphazard and random character of my interactions with individual team members in the work setting. In their responses, participants also indicated that they had particularly enjoyed the research interviews not least because it had afforded an opportunity to express their views, to 'let off steam' and to ventilate some of the anger and frustration they felt.

Thirdly, amongst the plethora of documents available to me, the most useful for research purposes was one known as 'the manual'. The manual, intended for use by team members, set out detailed guidelines on what were deemed to be appropriate care management practices.

However, it was, I think, the combined deployment of those data sources that enhanced my understanding of the multilayered character of care management practices. Thus, documentary evidence suggested that user needs were determined through the supposedly neutral application of 'objective' criteria. However, some observation and interview evidence suggested that it was not uncommon for decisions on eligibility to be constructed through opaque, highly individualized and sometimes arbitrary practitioner judgments which were then creatively disguised and reworked to 'fit' the eligibility criteria. Furthermore, whilst some interview data reflected formal practitioner perspectives and 'official speak', other interview and observation material highlighted significant points of dissonance between formal and informal practitioner positions. Observation data in particular provided important insights into how such tensions between proclaimed progressive values and oppressive everyday practices might be managed. The triangulated research processes therefore highlighted some of the strategies through which particular user/practitioner positions were constructed. Of particular significance in this context was the combined deployment of overt discourses of justification and covert discourses of application.

Notwithstanding, however, the positive benefits of the chosen research approach, the transformation of raw data into a credible research account raised a number of dilemmas that I now consider.

DATA ANALYSIS AND THE CONSTRUCTION OF A RESEARCH ACCOUNT

In this section, I outline problematic aspects of data analysis, strategies that facilitated their inevitably partial resolution and supportive influences that enabled me to complete the project.

In terms of interview material, I initially experienced difficulty in separating the interview contents from the interviewees I had come to know as individuals. The strategy I used to counter this was to try to focus wholly on the interview content and to segment, categorize and reassemble all the interview material in terms of concepts and themes. In attempting to deal with the mass of observation and interview data, I was aware of the perhaps all too often irresistible attraction of the colorful remark or comment that appeared to 'prove' my particular argument. I therefore tried to ensure that the evidence used to sustain my arguments was quantitatively substantive and not simply highly individual or idiosyncratic viewpoints.

However, in terms of constructing a reasonably coherent narrative from the 'messiness' of data, I think the single most useful strategy was to have a detailed written record of my observation and interview data. This record served as an invaluable aid to accurate recall of events and thus helped to prevent the creative reinvention or embellishment of either what happened or how particular events, statements and perspectives were understood or interpreted at the time. As a reflexive tool, reading and rereading my written material enabled me to reconsider my interpretation of events with the benefit of a degree of emotional detachment and critical distance from the events themselves.

In terms of ethical behavior, an ongoing concern was how to handle material gained in informal settings for whose use I could not claim to have explicit and specific participants' consent. Consequently, I limited the use of such material to what seemed absolutely necessary in order to illustrate particular arguments. Thus, paradoxically, while the insights gained through the observation process informed and shaped the contours of the research findings, the observation data did not appear to have an overarching significance in the research account. Furthermore, in presenting the findings, I exercised great care in order to ensure that as far as possible, the anonymity of both the participants and the research setting was preserved.

However, whatever strategies I used, I accept that, because knowledge is inseparable from the knower (Lincoln & Guba, 2000), what I chose to 'see' and take account of reflected my own particular interests and positions. Therefore, I argue that the research product did not simply emerge from the rigorous application of a set of technical procedures or ethical guidelines. Rather, I suggest that it was created through the continual if often unconscious interplay between my ideological standpoint, the themes as identified in the research questions, the thematic structures as constructed in the theoretical framework, the evidence as produced in the research data and my perceived responsibilities as a researcher. In the latter context, I hope that other researchers reading my field notes and interview transcripts would confirm that the evidence supported the description and analysis even if they did not necessarily agree with the conclusions reached.

Impact of and Influences on the Analysis and Writing-up Process

I think the often challenging, wearisome processes of analysis and writing-up were offset by productive individual and collective discussions with students and staff.

Such discussions enabled me to write a more considered and less superficial critique of the practices observed. Of key importance was continued guidance on the need to avoid a superior moral or cognitive tone, to look for 'difference' rather than homogenization in the research participants' positions and to recognize the relatively powerful position of the researcher when interpreting data and constructing findings. This guidance also encouraged me to focus on the varied, complex and contradictory strategies deployed by care managers in the course of their practice and to consider how those strategies appeared to make sense to them. Thus, to venture however cautiously or tentatively from the safety of binary certainties into the more risky, uncertain territories of overlapping, interconnected, contradictory and disjointed patterns of discursive positions was one of the more challenging but rewarding aspects of the research experience.

Nonetheless, the ultimate aims of the process were to identify and highlight the most significant research findings. In this context, it also seemed important to consider how the research experience influenced my own positions and perspectives. These are the questions I consider in the next section.

PERSONAL PERSPECTIVES AND RESEARCH FINDINGS

My post-research ideological position is a heightened critique of welfare practices and increased skepticism of the potential for transformative change within current structures of welfare provision. Furthermore, I am even more wary of 'quick fix', 'empowering' solutions that claim to address and redress the current power inequalities between disabled people who seek access to social care provision and the gatekeepers who decide on the validity or invalidity of such claims.

Such skepticism and wariness are fuelled by the apparent dominance of deficit disability and user discourses, the concomitant marginalized positioning of the social model and the apparent ease with which deficit user positions facilitated the construction of care managers as 'reliable experts' in the care management practices I observed. That such positions were accomplished within a disciplinary framework was evidenced by the subordinate positioning of the user in the assessment/ examination process, the ubiquity and intensity of the care management 'gaze' and the often covert modes of scrutiny and surveillance deployed in the normalizing processes of homogenization, differentiation, determination, individualization and exclusion through which the user 'case' was constructed.

Finally, the research highlighted the dominance of budgetary discourses in front-line practices. In this context, the positioning of practitioners as the subjects/objects of the disciplinary gaze, the objectified positioning of users as items of expenditure and the absence of users from decision-making fora, illustrated the hollowness of official commitments to social model-oriented and user-centered practices. However, for social modellists, it is not only the content but the potential usefulness of research that is a key concern. The next section addresses this question in relation to my research project.

USEFULNESS OF RESEARCH

With regard to the potential usefulness of the research, I fully accept that the project may be critiqued from a social model perspective for the lack of involvement of disabled people in its design, implementation and analysis. To the extent, however, that the aims of the research were to demystify oppressive structures and processes (Barnes, 1992), to turn 'the spotlight on the oppressors' (Morris, 1992, p. 165) and to focus attention on the relatively powerful (Riddell, Brown & Duffield, 1995), it may be argued that the research was at least emancipatory in intent. Furthermore, I consider that the research, albeit in a necessarily limited way indicated the ease with which the linguistic codes associated with social modellist/user-centered discourses may become enmeshed in practitioner narratives that sustain rather than challenge existing power/knowledge matrices. The research also highlighted the multidimensional character of disability/user discourses, the links between disability, impairment and bio-power and the potentially oppressive effects of discourses that position the 'ideal' able/disabled subject as independent.

In addition to the data produced, the research focus on practitioners posed a number of questions concerning who are/should be the researched and the identification of norms that might inform the research process. The research norms produced within an emancipatory paradigm include participant involvement in choice of topic (Vernon, 1997), the placing of control 'in the hands of the researched' (Oliver, 1997, p. 17) and identifying appropriate research aims in terms of 'reciprocity, gain and empowerment' (ibid.). There appears to be an implicit assumption underpinning such research norms, that the 'researched' are disabled people; that is those who have been or are the subjects/objects of oppressive practices. However, if it is accepted that those who exercise power over disabled people are a legitimate focus of emancipatory research, then it seems that research norms that privilege the researched need to be reconsidered. In such a context, the challenge seems to be to develop research practices which, whilst respectful of the rights and interests of the researched, bring to critical attention some of the oppressive practices in which they are engaged. To some extent, the research dilemmas and difficulties discussed in this chapter both reflect and attempt to address these very issues.

CONCLUSION

In drawing this chapter to a conclusion, I acknowledge some perceived inadequacies and unresolved questions related to the research project. I draw attention to what I consider to be the more significant research findings and I offer tentative suggestions for future directions of disability research.

One of the flaws in the project, as constructed, was the absence of any detailed or open discussion with participants on the substantive conclusions of the research. There are a number of grounds on which such lack of engagement may be rationalized. They include avoidance of potentially hostile responses to highly critical research findings, protection of the interests of both researcher and researched, possible breaches of confidentiality, or other unintended consequences. However, with hindsight, I consider that my failure to elicit and incorporate participants' responses to the research findings in the final account, constitutes one of the weaknesses of the research both in terms of ethical imperatives and the provision of richer and more complete data.

In terms of research outcomes, one of the unresolved questions is the typicality or otherwise of the discursive patterns, power relationships and disciplinary practices discussed in my research. A central concern in this context is whether I have been overconfident in assuming that what I found in a specific research site was broadly applicable to care management practices generally. I consider that the practices I highlighted were undoubtedly produced within dominant disability, professional and administrative discourses. However, I continue to question whether a combination or confluence of individual factors, organizational dysfunction, location in an economically disadvantaged area, resulted in local forms of practice that were particularly marked by practitioner defensiveness and negative constructions of users. In other words, would research in a different care management setting have produced broadly similar or significantly different results? It may be that such concerns reflect the specters of representativeness and replicability that haunt all single case studies and for which there are no easy answers.

However, despite its inadequacies and limitations, I contend that the research was purposeful, from a social model perspective, to the extent that I attempted to demonstrate how, under the camouflaging cover of social modellist and user-centered discourses, everyday institutional practices were produced within a power/knowledge matrix that positioned practitioners as 'expert' and disabled people as the unreliable 'other'. In terms of its approach, the research also attempted to invert the normative research binaries of service user visibility and practitioner invisibility.

With regard to further directions of disability research, this project points to a number of potentially fruitful areas of enquiry. My experience suggests that issues such as access, researcher positioning, disclosure of research aims and power relationships may assume particular significance when researching those who occupy relatively powerful positions. Furthermore, I argue that wherever on the oppressor/oppressed spectrum we place those we research, a reasonably satisfactory research outcome may depend on the development of empathetic relationships and inclusive practices with research participants at every stage of the research.

Despite the caveats concerning case study research I have already identified, I consider that this particular study highlights the need for a wider range of ethnographic studies or other field based research initiatives in the field of social care. Such initiatives seem particularly pressing given the paucity of similar studies, the 'gap' between official discourses proclaiming the centrality of user choice, voice and personalization in welfare provision and the bleak material reality of unmet demand, increasingly restrictive eligibility criteria and lack of resources. In broader terms, the research may also indicate the importance of gaining access to and developing better understanding of everyday practices, whose covert and opaque character may render them relatively immune from and inaccessible to critical interrogation, public scrutiny and political change. Whether in the field of medicine, social care or education, the most fertile focus of research may be institutions or practices that have traditionally been most resistant to critical ethnographic enquiry.

Finally, while aware of the risks of definitive conclusions based on fragmentary evidence, I hope that some of the ideas discussed in this paper may reach a wider audience and make a contribution to further research on and changes to practices that oppress disabled people.

REFERENCES

Adler, P. A., & Adler, P. (1994). Observational techniques. In N. Denzin & Y. S. Lincoln (Eds.), *Handbook of qualitative research* (pp. 377–392). London: Sage.

Allan, J. (1999). *Actively seeking inclusion: Pupils with special needs in mainstream schools*. London: Falmer Press.

Allan, J., & Slee, R. (2008). *Doing inclusive education research*. Rotterdam: Sense Publishers.

Bailey, R., & Brake, M. (Eds.). (1975). *Radical social work*. London: Edward Arnold.

Barnes, C. (1990). *'Cabbage syndrome': The social construction of dependence*. Basingstoke: The Falmer Press.

Barnes, C. (1992). Qualitative research: Valuable or irrelevant? *Disability, Handicap and Society, 7*(2), 115–124.

Barton, L. (1989). Introduction. In L. Barton (Ed.), *Disability and dependency* (pp. 1–5). Lewes: The Falmer Press.

Bines, H. (1995). Risk, routine and reward: Confronting personal and social constructs in research on special educational needs. In P. Clough & L. Barton (Eds.), *Making difficulties: Research and the construction of special educational needs* (pp. 42–58). London: Paul Chapman.

Burgess, R. G. (1987). *In the field: An introduction to field research*. London: Allen & Unwin.

Cameron, D. (2002). *Working with spoken discourse*. London: Sage.

Clarke, J. (1998). Thriving on chaos? Managerialism and social welfare. In J. Carter (Ed.), *Postmodernity and the fragmentation of welfare* (pp. 171–186). London: Routledge.

Clifford, J. (1986). Introduction: Partial truths. In J. Clifford & G. E. Marcus (Eds.), *Writing culture: The poetics and politics of ethnography* (pp. 1–26). Berkeley: University of California Press.

Cohen, L., & Manion, L. (1989). *Research methods in education*. London: Routledge.

Davis, J. M. (2006). Disability studies as ethnographic research and text: Research strategies and roles for promoting social change? In L. Barton (Ed.), *Overcoming disabling barriers: 18 years of Disability and Society* (pp. 307–324). Oxon: Routledge.

Dominelli, L., & McLeod, E. (1989). *Feminist social work*. London: Macmillan.

Entwistle, J. (1998). Sex/gender. In C. Jenks (Ed.) *Core sociological dichotomies* (pp. 151–165). London: Sage.

Foucault, M. (1980). Two lectures. In C. Gordon (Ed.), *Power/knowledge: Selected interviews and other writings 1972–1977* (pp. 80–108). Brighton: Harvester Press.

Foucault, M. (1982). The subject and power. In H. L. Dreyfus & P. Rabinow (Eds.), *Beyond structuralism and hermeneutics* (pp. 208–226). Hemel Hempstead: Harvester Press.

Foucault, M. (1988). Truth, power, self: An interview with Michel Foucault. In L. H. Martin, H. Gutman & P. H. Hutton (Eds.), *Technologies of the self: A seminar with Michel Foucault* (pp. 9–15). London: Tavistock.

Foucault, M. (1991a). *Discipline and punish: The birth of the prison*. London: Penguin Books.

Foucault, M. (1991b). The politics of health in the eighteenth century. In P. Rabinow (Ed.), *The Foucault reader* (pp. 273–289). London: Penguin Books.

Foucault, M., & Deleuze, G. (1977). Intellectuals and power. In D. F. Bouchard (Ed.), *Language, counter-memory, practice: Selected essays and interviews* (pp. 205–217). Ithaca: Cornell University Press.

Hallett, C. (1989). The gendered world of the social services department. In C. Hallett (Ed.), *Women and social services* (pp. 1–43). Hemel Hempstead: Harvester Wheatsheaf.

Healy, K. (2005). *Social work theories in context: Creating frameworks for practice*. Hampshire: Palgrave Macmillan.

Hey, V. (1997). *The company she keeps: An ethnography of girls' friendships*. Buckingham: Open University Press.

Johnson, J. M. (1975). *Doing field research*. New York: The Free Press.

Langan, M. (1998). The contested concept of need. In M. Langan (Ed.), *Welfare: Needs, rights and risks* (pp. 3–33). London: Routledge.

Lincoln, Y. S., & Guba, E. G. (2000). (2nd ed.). Paradigmatic controversies, contradictions and emerging confluences. In N. Denzin & Y. S. Lincoln (Eds.), *Handbook of qualitative research* (pp. 62–188). London: Sage.

Morris, J. (1991). *Pride against prejudice: A personal politics of disability*. London: The Women's Press.

Morris, J. (1992). Personal and political: A feminist perspective on researching physical disability. *Disability, Handicap and Society, 7*(2), 157–166.

Murphy, E., & Dingwall, R. (2001). The ethics of ethnography. In P. Atkinson, A. Coffey, S. Delamont, J. Lofland & L. Lofland (Eds.), *Handbook of ethnography* (pp. 339–351). London: Sage.

Newman, J. (1998). Managerialism and social welfare. In G. Hughes & G. Lewis (Eds.), *Unsettling welfare: The reconstruction of social policy* (pp. 333–374). London: Routledge & Kegan Paul.

Oliver, M. (1990). *The politics of disablement*. Basingstoke: Macmillan.

Oliver, M. (1997). Emancipatory research: Realistic goal or impossible dream? In C. Barnes & G. Mercer (Eds.), *Doing disability research* (pp. 15–31). Leeds: The Disability Press.

Oliver, M. (2004). If I had a hammer: The social model in action. In J. Swain, S. French, C. Barnes & C. Thomas (Eds.), *Disabling barriers – enabling environments* (2nd ed., pp. 7–12). London: Sage.

Oliver, M., & Barnes, C. (2012). *The new politics of disablement* (2nd ed.). Basingstoke: Palgrave Macmillan.

Phoenix, A. (1994). Practising feminist research: The intersection of gender and 'race' in the research process. In M. Maynard & J. Purvis (Eds.), *Researching women's lives from a feminist perspective* (pp. 49–71). London: Taylor & Francis.

Priestley, M. (1999). *Disability politics and community care*. London: Jessica Kingsley Publishers.

Riddell, S., Brown, S., & Duffield, J. (1995). The ethics of policy-focused research in special educational needs. In P. Clough & L. Barton (Eds.), *Making difficulties: Research and the construction of special educational needs* (pp. 42–58). London: Paul Chapman Publishing.

Sapsford, R., & Abbott, P. (1992). *Research methods for nurses and the caring professions*. Buckingham: Open University Press.

Satyamurti, C. (1981). *Occupational survival*. Oxford: Basil Blackwell.

Silverman, D. (2000). *Doing qualitative research*. London: Sage.

Simpkin, M. (1979). *Trapped within welfare: Surviving social work*. London: Macmillan.

Skeggs, B. (2001). Feminist ethnography. In P. Atkinson, A. Coffey, S. Delamont, J. Lofland & L. Lofland (Eds.), *Handbook of ethnography* (pp. 426–442). London: Sage.

Strauss, A., & Corbin, J. (1990). *Basics of qualitative research: Grounded theory procedures and techniques*. London: Sage.

Swain, J. (1995). Constructing participatory research: In principle and in practice. In P. Clough & L. Barton (Eds.), *Making difficulties: Research and the construction of special educational needs* (pp. 75–93). London: Paul Chapman Publishing.

Timms, N. (1964). *Social casework: Principles and practice*. London: Routledge & Kegan Paul.

Vernon, A. (1997). Reflexivity: The dilemmas of researching from the inside. In C. Barnes & G. Mercer (Eds.), *Doing disability research* (pp. 158–176). Leeds: The Disability Press.

Warren, C. A. B. (1988). *Gender issues in field research*. California: Sage.

Wilson, E. (1977). *Women and the welfare state*. London: Tavistock.

Yin, R. K. (1994). *Case study research: Design and methods*. London: Sage.

SIMONI SYMEONIDOU

4. RESEARCHING DISABILITY POLITICS: BEYOND THE SOCIAL MODEL AND BACK AGAIN

INTRODUCTION

As I begin to write this chapter, I recall a book edited by Clough and Corbett (2000), in which key academics of inclusive education reflected on their background experience, explaining their journey of researching and theorizing about disability. I remember how impressed I was to read Len Barton's first meaningful encounter with disabled people when he accepted a job as a teacher of woodwork and swimming for children classified as having learning difficulties: he was motivated by the feeling that disabled children needed somebody like him ('Christian-informed pressure', Barton, 2000, p. 51). I also remember how amazed I was to discover that like Len Barton, other key figures of inclusive education (who had influenced numerous university students, disabled activists, academics and other disability related groups), were not always in the inclusive track and on the contrary, they were in the exact opposite direction. There seemed to be something influential about the social model of disability that acted as a turning point to their thinking and research. Even those who criticize or reject the social model may not deny that it *did* influence their personal journey in the field and this is what seems to have happened to me.

As a teenager, I remember operating on the basis of the charity model and thinking according to the medical model. This ideology was expected, given that the Greek-Cypriot culture, in which I grew up, had a traditional approach to disability based on segregation, medicalization and charity (Symeonidou, 2009a). As a high school student, I became an active volunteer of the RadioMarathon, the biggest annual charity fiesta for 'children with special needs' in Cyprus. During the two days of the event, I was out in the central avenues of Nicosia, wearing the RadioMarathon t-shirt and collecting money for 'those' children. At night, I slept with a pocket sized radio next to my pillow, listening to pitiful spots with parents talking about their children with 'special abilities' and how important it was to collect money in order to help them live a better life. Their stories, followed by the sentimental comments of the radio producers, sometimes made me cry, but when they reported on how well we were doing with collecting more money than in the previous year, I smiled again. At the end of the fiesta, I was pleased because I had done something to help children 'in need'.

These experiences explain why I soon expressed a desire to become a speech therapist: I was fascinated by the fact that apart from fundraising, I could help

S. Symeonidou and K. Beauchamp-Pryor (Eds.), Purpose, Process and Future Direction of Disability Research, 45–58.

children through my profession. Although I yearned to become a speech therapist, I changed my journey and studied Primary Education at the University of Cyprus. This was because the teaching profession is one of the most prestigious and well-paid professions in Cyprus, plus on graduation, you are immediately appointed as a teacher for public schools (at least this was the case at the time I graduated). Therefore, teaching is usually a parents' dream-field of study for their children. Thus, I developed a plan: if I passed the entrance examinations (a difficult task) and became a teacher (not so difficult once you are enrolled), I would pursue further studies in speech therapy abroad. I was accepted at the local university and I became a primary education teacher, but after I graduated, speech therapy was no longer on my 'to-do' list.

In this chapter, I critically reflect on my encounters with the social model of disability and I discuss the way in which it influenced important research decisions. I consider the dilemmas the social model introduced into my PhD research in terms of the most appropriate theoretical framework and research paradigm. Finally, I explain how the social model and ideas became central to my research and teaching choices.

ENCOUNTER WITH THE SOCIAL MODEL OF DISABILITY

My first encounter with the social model of disability was at the University of Cyprus where I studied Primary Education (1994–98) and I followed the specialization route of Inclusive Education (three modules). In the absence of local literature about disability issues at the time, our instructors (none of whom were local) familiarized us with literature from the UK and the USA. I was impressed by the richness of traditions and ideas in the field, and was particularly influenced by Helen Phtiaka. She introduced us to the work of key authors of inclusive education (specifically: Barton, 1988, *Politics of special educational needs*; Tomlinson, 1992, *Sociology of special education*) and she engaged us in critical reflections between their work and educational developments in Cyprus (Phtiaka, 1999).

I graduated from the University of Cyprus, aware of the inclusive education approach and its relationship with the social model of disability. It was from this position that I moved to the University of Manchester for postgraduate studies. My theoretical background enabled me to identify fundamental links between basic disability studies ideas and key inclusive education ideas. For example, the medical and the social model of disability (at the heart of disability studies) shared common ground with important approaches developed in inclusive education: the individual pupil approach (Hart, 1986) is based upon similar issues to those focused on within a medical model position, for instance individual 'inability' and 'inadequacy' and meeting 'needs'; whereas the school improvement approach (Booth, Ainscow, Black-Hawkins, Vaughan & Shaw, 1999) raised similar issues to those addressed within the social model, for instance identifying those barriers resulting from the environment.

I was fascinated by the possibilities of conducting research in inclusive education driven by the social model. Nevertheless, the nature of the masters program was more relevant to the curriculum and school improvement approach. My supervisor was Mel Ainscow, a renowned academic for his work in school improvement. I remember that when I prepared my dissertation proposal, I experienced a dilemma that troubled me for several days (and nights): I wanted to combine disability studies research with inclusive education research, but thought that my supervisor's research interests and valuable experience in school improvement initiatives were not on par with what I wanted to do. Initially, I did not share my dilemma with him and instead suggested a research proposal reflecting his research profile. However, a couple of days later I went back to his office suggesting an alternative research project concerning disabled people's perspectives about developments in education policy: to my surprise and delight, Mel Ainscow agreed with my proposed new topic. My research experience had strengthened my position that disabled people's views about education needed to be focused upon and it convinced me that there were essential links between inclusive education and disability studies.

On my return to Cyprus, I started work in primary education, but I kept exploring a wide range of literature in order to shape my theoretical background further and prepare for my PhD studies. It was during this time that I fortunately came across a book by Campbell and Oliver (1996), which acted as a source of inspiration for my PhD research proposal. Through interviews with disabled people, the protagonists of the British disability movement, the authors presented an account of the rise of disability politics in the UK. Interestingly, the authors were central figures of the movement themselves and they researched their collective history from within, reflecting on the process and on subsequent conceptualizations of disability and disability issues. Having read this book and recognized the value of their work, I realized the importance of carrying out a similar study in Cyprus. Apart from the obvious lack of any piece of disability studies research in Cyprus, it was difficult to explain why I wanted to take this journey: I was a non-disabled teacher graduate (well equipped with the inclusive education principles and literature), who had a desire to investigate the development of the disability movement in the Greek-Cypriot culture. With hindsight, the driving force was the impact of the social model of disability on my views: it changed my way of thinking and made me critical about social, political and educational issues.

BEYOND THE SOCIAL MODEL

Perhaps, one of the most important particularities of my PhD thesis[1] (Symeonidou, 2005) is the fact that in setting my theoretical framework, I positioned my research beyond the social model of disability: an odd decision given the fact that I was setting out to research disability politics.

During the first year of my PhD studies at the University of Cambridge, I attended research classes, I delved deeper in the disability studies literature and I initiated a dialogue around my readings with my other supervisor, Lesley Dee, who was not a disability studies scholar, but who was extremely keen to go along this path with me. It was from this position that I was able to think about my intended research project more thoroughly. As is usually the case, one author led me to another and existing ideas and beliefs were refined or even rejected in the light of new concepts and arguments. Initially, I was familiar with the medical and social models as well as the materialist approach to disability (Oliver, 1990; Oliver & Barnes, 2012), but my knowledge extended to include feminist (Thomas, 1999) and postmodern/ poststructural ideas (Corker & Shakespeare, 2002) about disability. These ideas opened other fronts of thinking and encouraged me to think about disability from multiple perspectives. The concepts of personal experience of disability, the contested meaning of impairment and the significance of culture and history functioned as new areas of interest.

Given this framework, I scrutinized my original decision to merely record the historical development of the disability movement. My research aims reflected my intention to research several issues related to disability and disability politics. In particular, the first aim was to explore the experience of disability and disability politics in the context of Cyprus. My questions included: What did it mean to be disabled in Cyprus? What did it mean to be a disabled activist in Cyprus? Were these experiences interrelated and in what way? I pursued this aim through in-depth oral history interviews with key disabled activists. I chose to focus on key disabled activists as I came to believe that they represented a group of people who, despite the richness of experiences at a personal and political level, remained outside the sphere of disability research. My second aim was to conceptualize disabled activists' understandings of their experience by placing it in a historical perspective and in the culturally specific context of Cyprus. Therefore, how could history and culture help interpret the experience of disability and disability politics, and how was the development of the Greek-Cypriot disability movement related to the general historical and cultural context of Cyprus?

Although I acknowledged that the social model and the approaches that followed (materialist, feminist, postmodern/poststructuralist) contributed to disability theory in complementary ways, I decided to position my study within feminism and postmodernism. This was not because I rejected the social model or the materialist and poststructuralist explanations of disability, nor because I labeled myself as feminist, postmodernist or postmodern feminist. Rather, I decided to engage in this process believing that feminism and postmodernism might be helpful in conceptualizing disability and disability politics in the context of Cyprus. Having decided upon this approach, my theoretical framework was shaped as follows: the personal experience of disability can be positioned and conceptualized within the contexts of feminism (personal experience of impairment and disability) and postmodernism (culture, history and identity); and disability politics can be conceptualized through the feminist maxim that 'the personal is political' and the postmodern assumption that politics need no reliance upon theory or grand narratives. As my research sought to understand how disability and disability politics were experienced and conceptualized in a particular cultural context, where disability theory and political disability models were absent, I considered that feminism and postmodernism provided a rich framework to inform my study and its contribution to theory at local and global level.

My decision to locate my research in feminism and postmodernism was not without limitations. These theoretical standpoints brought into my research many contested concepts (identity, gender, impairment) which needed to be understood within the complex context of Cyprus. Furthermore, the critiques about the epistemological and methodological limitations of postmodernism made my task more difficult. The focus of postmodernism on culture, although a strength for my research, could easily be transformed to a limitation if I restricted my understandings of disability to the Greek-Cypriot context. Thus, balancing cross-cultural understandings of disability and disability politics with my attempts to understand and explain the local was a constant worry. Furthermore, my focus on history needed to be addressed with caution to avoid criticism of disengaging the past from the present, which is an important criticism of Foucault's work (Sarup, 1993). Criticism of Foucault's work informed my methodological decisions which will be explained later in this chapter. Last but not least, I was aware that feminists might criticize me for trying to combine feminism and postmodernism in this type of research, as they reject the relevance of postmodernist thinking to politics (Fraser & Nicholson, 1990). However, I concluded that developing such a framework might help me balance postmodernists' arguments about politics without a general theory, with the social model proponents' arguments.

Another important concern which related to my theoretical framework was its potential to facilitate my conceptualizations of identity. The concept of identity is complex as it has various distinctions and definitions (Crossley, 2002; Giddens, 2001; Johnston, Laraña & Gusfield, 1994; Melucci, 1995; Sarup, 1996). Through my theoretical framework, I planned to explore the feminist assumption that there was a relationship between the personal and the political experience of disabled people through identity. Besides, among disability theorists there were calls for the importance of focusing on the personal experience of disability and its relationship with political action (Corker & French, 1999; Morris, 1991), a relationship that I sought to explore. At the same time, the way collective identity is understood within postmodernism seemed problematic as postmodernists challenge the development of 'the disabled identity' (Shakespeare, 2006). A consistent postmodernist would argue that collective identities reproduce the knowledge/power relationships and maintain the gap between the 'Self' and the 'Other'. At the other end of the continuum, the proponents of the social model insist that without a collective identity, disability politics is impossible (Campbell & Oliver, 1996). In this context, issues about the construction of identity, the interaction of different types of identities (personal, group and collective) and the relationship between identity, difference and activism became significant.

SETTLING ON THE MOST APPROPRIATE RESEARCH PARADIGM

Given the research aims and the theoretical framework, I made a series of methodological decisions, and of these, I mark out the choice of research paradigm as the hardest decision of this phase.

Considering the realization that researching disability is a contested issue, the process of arriving at a decision about my research paradigm became a source of stress. The questions of who disability research aims to serve and what is the role of non-disabled researchers were central in contemporary debates. A group of disability theorists, mainly disabled activists/academics who strongly believed that disability research should reflect the goals of the disability movement, called for the adoption of an emancipatory research paradigm, arguing that this best serves the interests of disabled people (Barnes, 2003; Barnes & Mercer, 1997; Oliver, 1992; 1997; Zarb, 1992; 1997). Other scholars, who considered themselves accountable both to the disability movement and to the academy, increasingly recognized the importance of other research paradigms in conceptualizing both disability and disability politics (Goodley, Lawthom, Clough & Moore, 2004; Shakespeare, 2006; Thomas, 1999).

According to Mercer (2002), the emancipatory research paradigm relies upon: adherence to the social model of disability (and the rejection of the medical model); adoption of a partisan research approach (one that denies researcher's objectivity and neutrality) in order to facilitate disabled people's political struggles; rejection of the traditional researcher-researched hierarchy; and pluralism of choice in methodologies and methods. Within this context, the following question became crucial: Should I locate my research in the emancipatory paradigm in the way this is understood by a group of disabled activists who are committed to the social model of disability? The answer was not clear cut as many issues arose to the contrary. For example, my theoretical framework did not involve the social model, although I was committed to the principles of the social model and I was definitely rejecting the medical model of disability. Regarding the researcher-researched relationship, I was not prepared to abandon the researcher's autonomy and the role of controlling the research. This would be extremely difficult, given my inexperience in research projects of that scale and the general context of my research (a PhD project with a set duration and a series of decisions that needed to be taken by the student researcher).

Thus, I decided that my study was not falling in the emancipatory research paradigm, even though I believed that it was emancipatory for disabled people in many ways. First, the intention of my research was to ensure that disabled people's voices were heard, an important prerequisite of empowerment; and second, as a non-disabled independent researcher I did not favour any individual or impairment group. Research wise, this was an advantage as it positively influenced all steps of the process, such as sampling (decisions about who to include and exclude), analysis (how to interpret the different stories) and findings (how to construct the researcher's story in a way that is meaningful to the group researched); third, as a researcher influenced by inclusive education and disability studies, I had the opportunity to design the research in ways that made it useful for groups linked to both disciplines. For example, the emphasis on the lived experience of disabled people in the local culture was useful for teacher education and the interplay between identities within the disability movement was important for the future involvement of disabled activists in politics; and last, but not least, I appreciated Michael Oliver's (1997) realization that it might not be possible to fully implement emancipatory research and a statement by Barnes (2003), that a great deal of valuable disability research had been undertaken, even though it cannot be characterized as emancipatory.

My encounter with the hermeneutic paradigm dragged me to another direction (once again). Hermeneutics is an interpretive paradigm and does not fall within critical theory, which theoretically is closer to the emancipatory paradigm. However, I realized that the hermeneutic paradigm was valuable for the type of research I intended to carry out. Hermeneutics refers to the art, theory and philosophy of the interpretation of meaning ascribed to an object (Schwandt, 1997). Arguably, for the hermeneutical scholar there can be no final interpretation as the data can be reinterpreted from different angles (Usher, 1996). Linked to this realization is the assumption that both the researcher and what is being researched (for example, text, human action, spoken utterances) are engaged in interpretations. In the case of oral narratives, for instance, the researcher needs to interpret the narratives, which are themselves the products of the respondents' interpretations of past experience, beliefs, and so forth. In hermeneutics, the interpretation always takes place against a background of assumptions and presuppositions, and beliefs and practices of which the subjects and the objects are never fully aware and can never be specified (Usher, 1996). Given that each researcher can focus on different aspects of the different perspectives revealed by the data (Goodson & Sikes, 2001), the argument that there is no final interpretation is further justified.

These assumptions were helpful in my research as I sought to understand a variety of experiences both at the personal and political level, in the multifaceted cultural and historical context of Cyprus. According to Hall (1995), as cited in Barton and Armstrong (1999), cultures are not internally coherent and even though they help to construct people's identities, their 'sameness' is not guaranteed. Indeed, in the Greek-Cypriot context, 'sameness' is defined through internal cultural differences. These differences play a central role in the formation of national identities which, when seen as a whole lead us, like hermeneutics, to multiple realities and multiple truths. This complexity is reflected in the respondents who bring to the cultural context their own differences stemming from their experience of disability. Subsequently, their experience of disability is different and is dependent upon various factors, such as gender, age, and type of impairment. Thus, the complexity embedded in my culturally specific disability research justified the adoption of hermeneutics.

Upon deciding to locate my study in hermeneutics, I revisited the issue of the researcher-researched relationship, raised by the proponents of the emancipatory research approach. Being a non-disabled researcher endeavoring to research disabled people increased my level of ethical responsibility towards my respondents. I was urged on considering power relations in order that a system of domination and oppression of disabled people was not reproduced through research. According to Stone and Priestley (1996), non-disabled researchers face the danger of conducting research that can be oppressive for disabled people, as similarly evidenced when men are researching women. Arguably, both disabled people and women conduct research differently from non-disabled people and men respectively, as they bring with them their experience of oppression. In this context, being a young non-disabled woman researcher raised several issues: I was fully aware of the fact that had my research been conducted by a male, mature, key disabled activist of the movement, the approach might have been totally different. However, I expressed my commitment in taking research decisions that were not oppressive to disabled people. Furthermore, while analyzing my data and writing-up, I was guided by my decision to prepare an empowering research account for disabled people in direct and indirect ways.

MAKING MEANING BY INTERPRETING STORIES

In ideal research projects, epistemology fits neatly with the preferred research approach and analysis, albeit this was not the case for my project. In their life story research projects, Goodley et al. (2004) attempted to show the link between epistemology, research approach and analysis in four straightforward projects. They showed how a poststructuralist epistemology fitted with a non-participatory research approach and discourse analysis (Dan Goodley), how a feminist epistemology complied with an emancipatory interview approach and a voice relational analysis (Rebecca Lawthom), how a social model epistemology fitted with a participatory ethnography and grounded theory (Michele Moore) and how a literary theory epistemology linked with non-participatory fiction approach and literary criticism (Peter Clough). However, as is often the case, different concerns may mean that there can be no direct link between a given epistemology and a directly resulting approach to analysis (Goodley et al., 2004). Locating my study in the theoretical frameworks of feminism and postmodernism, but maintaining the position that I did not intend to directly emancipate disabled people (feminist research approach) or focus exclusively on grand and alternative narratives or discourses (postmodernist/ poststructuralist research approaches), called for some rigorous thinking about my research approach. The decision to take a hermeneutical research approach and the use of oral history interviews and documents helped bridge the gap between feminist and postmodernist epistemologies as it enabled a joint focus: a focus on disabled people's voice and the personal on the one hand, and on the other, a focus on localized personal and political experiences, on local alternative narratives and partly, on power relations and discourse.

The choice of hermeneutics facilitated the combination of more than one analytical trend. In my analysis, I adopted a grounded theory approach marked by voice relational approach. Following a grounded theory approach, I organized the findings in a way so that I narrated some interrelated 'stories': the story of the cultural and materialist forces which shaped the oppression experienced by disabled people in the context of Cyprus; the personal experience of individuals in education, employment, intimate relationships and marriage, and their responses to acquired impairments; the historical (albeit interpretive) understanding of the development of the disability movement in Cyprus (followed by a discussion of the interplay of identities and gender in the disability movement); and the political experience of disabled activists through their experience in single-impairment and collective organizations respectively. Importantly, documents and oral history interviews were integrally linked throughout the process. Within this context, voice relational approach was helpful as it enabled me to interpret the data through different standpoints (Brown & Gilligan, 1992; Finch, 1984; Riessman, 1993). Goodley et al. (2004) note that this type of analysis takes the form of a number of readings of the narrative, such as: reading for the plot and our responses to the narrative; reading for the voice of 'I'; reading for relationships; and placing people within cultural and social structures. These principles were central in my effort to analyze the stories of the respondents, in order to achieve the best possible interpretation. Inevitably, I occasionally drew upon poststructuralist approaches when I conceptualized people's stories through the concepts of the 'Self' and the 'Other'. As I was engaged in theory building, the feminist and, at cases, the poststructuralist analytical stances were not presented separately; rather, the reader was left to detect these analytical features as they were blended in the text.

The task of interpretation was bounded upon serious consideration for several reasons. The first of these was the dilemma of how far a researcher can go in interpreting people's stories: Is the researcher in a position to be certain about interpretation? Although different researchers interpret the same stories in different ways, I found myself in the position of having to be careful of any interpretation and argument I developed. Sometimes, I was not certain about several issues and the only remedy was to explore alternative ways of thinking and interpreting. Linked to this was the consent by respondents for non-anonymity, which was an asset for my research and the group researched because it enabled the writing of a historical account of a group whose voice is usually under represented (Tonkin, 1992; Yow, 1994). However, not disguising the respondents whilst writing-up proved demanding and ethical issues were at the centre of analysis. It was important for me, as it is for any researcher, to feel free to form a critical account of the issues being researched. An honest critical account is also important for the audience of the research, who are entitled to such an account. However, a trade off between freedom of the researcher and non-anonymity was unavoidable. I repeatedly found myself in situations where I needed to take decisions about including or omitting certain quotations because I had to consider the consequences of each decision. For example, there were cases where including a quotation would be offensive to other respondents; moreover, it would not add to my interpretation. The criterion which guided me was the importance of each piece of information for the respondents, the research and the field.

As I began to draw out of the data common themes and patterns, I began to create a meaningful story. Through my engagement at a higher level of theory building I was able to draw the connections with broader explanations and theories. Apart from the literature, my interaction with disability studies scholars at conferences and meetings in the UK and the feedback received from disabled activists in Cyprus were useful to the development of my thinking within the ongoing process of making meaning.

BEYOND THE SOCIAL MODEL AND BACK AGAIN: THE UNFINISHED
BUSINESS OF RESEARCH

The end of my research was marked by an improved theoretical model based on feminism and postmodernism, albeit marked by the social model of disability. In particular, the individual experience of disability was influenced by the personal, social and national identities which made up the Greek-Cypriot identity; experience influenced by the cultural and historical particularities of Cyprus, such as nationalism, religion, charity, patriarchy, family, colonization, invasion, and Western superiority. Within this context, the development of the disability movement in Cyprus was strongly influenced by its members' personal experience of disability in the given culture. The involvement of activists in disability politics was strongly related with their aspirations to meet personhood (to become 'well-educated' individuals, to secure a 'decent' job, to have a family of their own and to enjoy a good social life). For historical and social reasons, single-impairment organizations initially pursued these goals. As a result, the main feature of the disability movement was about strong group identities (developed within single-impairment organizations), lack of theory or model (the social model) to guide collective activism and absence of collective identity (the disabled identity). Thus, the initial theoretical model was proved useful in verifying that postmodernism and feminism provided a useful framework for understanding and theorizing disability. With regard to disability, both feminism and postmodernism were useful. Feminism was important for its adherence to the personal experience of disability and postmodernism for its calls to conceptualize disability within a given culture, history and language. As far as disability politics were concerned, the feminist maxim that 'the personal is political' was an extremely illuminating dimension to comprehend disability politics in Cyprus, whereas the assumption of postmodernism that theories and grand narratives was not helpful in politics was not applicable in the case of the disability movement. Put simply, the absence of the social model of disability in Cyprus acted as a check for powerful disability politics.

Upon the completion of my PhD and my return to Cyprus, I was anxious that my research made a real impact for the group researched. I initially expected my research to act as a key historical document for the disability movement, one that narrated an important collective story and illuminated the future struggles of disabled activists in politics. I now grasp the counsel of Allan and Slee that we need to remember that our research 'occupies just a small place in the world' and it is better 'not to hope for too much, too soon' (2008, p. 101). In the years that followed, my research did have an impact, but not in the ways I originally anticipated. For example, it was meaningful for a number of disabled activists who conceptualized it in ways that suited their thoughts and worries at the time they came across to my writings. I was thrilled to witness that after having read my research, one of the participants of the study began to consider the importance of engaging with theoretical readings about disability and to record his experiences in the single-impairment organization and in the disability movement. To this end, he initiated a dialogue with me, requesting basic disability studies literature and then went on to design a research project, which he now carries out. His endeavor was extremely rewarding given the absence of any interest about disability studies and the disability studies literature in Cyprus (Symeonidou, 2009b). Furthermore, a kind of basic dialogue amongst disabled activists was initiated in local conferences and radio stations where I presented part of the research findings.

On another development, my research became central in the approach I developed in teacher education for inclusion courses at undergraduate, postgraduate and in-service training level. As a teacher educator, I developed a merged approach to teaching student teachers about inclusion, through inclusive education and disability studies literature (Symeonidou & Damianidou, 2012; Symeonidou & Phtiaka, 2009; 2012a; 2012b). The focus involved exposing students to the traditional medical and charity forces which constructed the concept of disability in Cyprus and their critical reflection upon the impact of oppressive conceptualizations of disability to the personal experience of disability in Cyprus. The following issues were discussed in the context of inclusive education: In what ways is the social model of disability useful in everyday decisions and interactions at class and at school level? How can we contribute to the removal of all barriers (for instance, attitudinal, curricular, and so on) to provide quality education of all children? How can we employ disabled people's culture in our endeavor? These questions are now at the centre of authors trying to incorporate the social model and disability studies ideas in teacher education for inclusion (for example, Baglieri, 2008; Ballard, 2003; Peters & Reid, 2009; Shapiro & Baglieri, 2010; Ware, 2007).

Even though 'my' research project resulted in a journey travelling 'beyond the social model and back again' and the findings began to fill a gap in the local (and perhaps the international) literature, the outcome does not signify the end of disability research. As we move on, developments in thinking alongside political developments at several levels (for instance, education, social policy and activism) necessitate revisiting old and new ideas through research to inform theory and practice regarding the future of disabled people. In Cyprus, there are currently important issues which stem either from traditional practices or from new trends, which need to be researched further. Firstly, the implementation of the *International classification of functioning, disability and health* (ICF) (World Health Organization, 2001) is top priority for the Department for Social Inclusion of Persons with Disabilities (part of the Ministry of

Employment), despite the expressed disagreement of the disability movement with the philosophy of ICF and the dangers inherent in using it either for the assessment of impairment and disability or for the adaptation of social policy. Secondly, services for disabled children and adults continue to be segregated from all mainstream services and they empower 'specialists' with medical conceptualizations of disability rather than disabled people. For example, the Ministry of Education and Culture presents 'special education' as a distinct branch, one that follows the departments of primary, secondary and higher education (Ministry of Education and Culture, 2012a), while at the same time it appears closely related to the department of primary education (Ministry of Education and Culture, 2012b). 'Special' schools, 'special' settings within mainstream schools, 'special' teaching staff, 'special' inspectors for 'special' teaching staff – all function independently in a segregating educational system. Researchers need to be aware of the interrelationships between disability matters which may, at a first glance, appear distinct. Through their research, they need to keep unraveling the existing gap between the well-being of disabled people and systems or policies developed by state bureaucrats who proclaim to serve 'equality', 'fairness' and 'human rights'.

RESEARCH JOURNEY

Personal research journeys are a valuable process for individuals. They often entail all the phases of a journey to a destination for the first time: choosing a place which looks interesting, planning ahead, preparing your suitcase according to weather conditions, going by the guide book at the beginning, leaving the book aside to explore new interesting places later on, putting information together to find your way in interesting cities or villages, discovering places which were not in your initial agenda, meeting interesting people that you may never forget, tasting new flavors, drinking new spirits, dancing with the locals, and when it is time to return home, rushing to the airport with such a heavy luggage that can hardly be moved, returning back home with new images and ideas in your head and looking forward to trying out some of the new cooking ideas you came across, without forgetting to add some of your favorite local spices of course. All journeys are unique in one way or another, and in the same way, the research journey I narrated reflected a personal and distinctive journey, which I hope I managed to convey. I also hope that my journey and its outcomes had an impact on other individuals and groups with a strong commitment to conceptualizing disability issues. However, a phrase on a poster at the local airport reminded me of this simple but wise acknowledgement: the best trip is always the next one.

NOTE

[1]   The findings from my doctoral study will be available in a forthcoming book to be published by Pedio Books.

REFERENCES

Allan, J., & Slee, R. (2008). *Doing inclusive education research.* Rotterdam: Sense Publishers.

Baglieri, S. (2008). 'I connected': Reflection and biography in teacher learning toward inclusion. *International Journal of Inclusive Education, 12*(5–6), 585–604.

Ballard, K. (2003). The analysis of context: Some thoughts on teacher education, culture, colonization and inequality. In T. Booth, K. Nes & M. Strømstad (Eds.), *Developing Inclusive Teacher Education* (pp. 59–77). London: RoutledgeFalmer.

Barnes, C. (2003). What difference a decade makes: Reflections on doing 'emancipatory' disability research. *Disability and Society, 18*(1), 3–17.

Barnes, C., & Mercer, G. (1997). Breaking the mould? An introduction to doing disability research. In C. Barnes & G. Mercer (Eds.), *Doing disability research* (pp. 1–14). Leeds: The Disability Press.

Barton, L. (2000). Profile: Len Barton. In P. Clough & J. Corbett (Eds.), *Theories of inclusive education* (pp. 51–54). London: Paul Chapman Publishing.

Barton, L. (Ed.). (1988). *The politics of special educational needs.* Lewes: The Falmer Press.

Barton, L., & Armstrong, F. (1999). Introduction. In F. Armstrong & L. Barton (Eds.), *Disability, human rights and education. Cross-cultural perspectives* (pp. 1–6). Buckingham: Open University Press.

Booth, T., Ainscow, M., Black-Hawkins, K., Vaughan, M., & Shaw, L. (1999). *Index for inclusion: Developing learning and participation in schools.* Bristol: CSIE.

Brown, L. M., & Gilligan, C. (1992). *Meeting at the crossroads: Women's psychology and girls' development.* Harvard: Harvard University Press.

Campbell, J., & Oliver, M. (1996). *Disability politics. Understanding our past, changing our future.* London: Routledge.

Clough, P., & Corbett, J. (Eds.). (2000). *Theories of inclusive education.* London: Paul Chapman Publishing.

Corker, M., & French, S. (1999). Reclaiming discourse in disability studies. In M. Corker & S. French (Eds.), *Disability discourse* (pp. 1–11). Buckingham: Open University Press.

Corker, M., & Shakespeare, T. (2002). Mapping the terrain. In M. Corker & T. Shakespeare (Eds.), *Disability/postmodernity. Embodying disability theory* (pp. 1–17). London: Continuum.

Crossley, N. (2002). *Making sense of social movements.* Buckingham: Open University Press.

Finch, J. (1984). It's great to have someone to talk to: The ethics and politics of interviewing women. In C. Bell & H. Roberts (Eds.), *Social researching: Politics, problems, practice* (pp. 70–87). London: Routledge and Kegan Paul.

Fraser, N., & Nicholson, L. (1990). Social criticism without philosophy: An encounter between feminism and postmodernism. In L. Nicholson (Ed.), *Feminism/postmodernism* (pp. 19–38). New York: Routledge.

Giddens, A. (2001). *Sociology.* Cambridge: Polity Press.

Goodley, D., Lawthom, R., Clough, P., & Moore, M. (2004). *Researching life stories: Method, theory and analyses in a biographical age.* London: RoutledgeFalmer.

Goodson, I., & Sikes, P. (2001). *Life history research in educational settings. Learning from lives.* Buckingham: Open University Press.

Hart, S. (1986). Evaluating support teaching. *Gnosis, 9,* 26–31.

Johnston, H., Laraña, E., & Gusfield, J. R. (1994). Identities, grievances and new social movements. In E. Laraña, H. Johnston & J. R. Gusfield (Eds.), *New social movements: From ideology to identity* (pp. 3–35). Philadelphia: Temple University Press.

Melucci, A. (1995). The process of collective identity. In H. Johnston & B. Klandermans (Eds.), *Social movements and culture.* London: UCL Press.

Mercer, G. (2002). Emancipatory disability research. In C. Barnes, M. Oliver & L. Barton (Eds.), *Disability studies today* (pp. 228–249). Cambridge: Polity.

Ministry of Education and Culture (2012a). *Educational system.* Retrieved May 26, 2012, from http://www.moec.gov.cy/en/

Ministry of Education and Culture (2012b). *Department of Primary Education.* Retrieved May 26, 2012, from http://www.moec.gov.cy/dde/en/index.html

Morris, J. (1991). *Pride against prejudice.* London: The Women's Press.

Oliver, M. (1990). *The politics of disablement.* Basingstoke: Macmillan.
Oliver, M. (1992). Changing the social relations of research production? *Disability and Society, 7*(2), 101–114.
Oliver, M. (1997). Emancipatory research: Realistic goal or impossible dream? In C. Barnes & G. Mercer (Eds.), *Doing disability research* (pp. 15–31). Leeds: The Disability Press.
Oliver, M., & Barnes, C. (2012). *The new politics of disablement* (2nd ed.). Basingstoke: Palgrave Macmillan.
Peters, S., & Reid, K. (2009). Resistance and discursive practice: Promoting advocacy in teacher undergraduate and graduate programmes. *Teaching and Teacher Education, 25*(4), 551–558.
Phtiaka, H. (1999). Disability, human rights and education in Cyprus. In F. Armstrong & L. Barton (Eds.), *Disability, human rights and education: Cross-cultural perspective* (pp. 176–192). Buckingham: Open University Press.
Riessman, C. K. (1993). *Narrative analysis.* Newbury Park: Sage Publications.
Sarup, M. (1993). *An introductory guide to poststructuralism and postmodernism.* New York: Harvester Wheatsheaf.
Sarup, M. (1996). *Identity, culture and the postmodern world.* Edinburgh: Edinburgh University Press.
Schwandt, T. A. (1997). *Qualitative inquiry. A dictionary of terms.* California: Sage.
Shakespeare, T. (2006). *Disability rights and wrongs.* London: Routledge.
Shapiro, A., & Baglieri, S. (2010). *Disability studies and the inclusive classroom.* London: Routledge.
Stone, E., & Priestley, M. (1996). Parasites, pawns and patterns: Disability research and the role of non-disabled researchers. *British Journal of Sociology, 47*(4), 699–716.
Symeonidou, S. (2005). *Understanding and theorising disability and disability politics: The case of the Cypriot disability movement.* PhD thesis. School of Education. University of Cambridge.
Symeonidou. S. (2009a). Trapped in our past: The price we have to pay for our cultural disability inheritance. *International Journal of Inclusive Education, 13*(6), 565–579.
Symeonidou. S. (2009b). The experience of disability activism through the development of the disability movement: How do disabled activists find their way in politics? *Scandinavian Journal of Disability Research, 11*(1), 17–34.
Symeonidou, S., & Damianidou, E. (2012). Enriching the subject of Greek Literature with the experience of the 'Other': an approach that fosters citizenship education in Cyprus. *International Journal of Inclusive Education,* DOI: 10.1080/13603116.2012.717638
Symeonidou, S., & Phtiaka, H. (2009). Using teachers' prior knowledge, attitudes and beliefs to develop in-service teacher education courses for inclusion. *Teaching and Teacher Education, 25*(4), 543–550.
Symeonidou, S., & Phtiaka, H. (2012a). *Εκπαίδευση για την ένταξη: από την έρευνα στην πράξη [Teacher education for inclusion: From research to praxis].* Athens: Pedio Books.
Symeonidou, S., & Phtiaka, H. (2012b). 'My colleagues wear blinkers... If they were trained, they would understand better'. Reflections on teacher education on inclusion in Cyprus. *Journal of Research in Special Educational Needs,* DOI: 10.1111/j.1471-3802.2012.01234.x
Thomas, C. (1999). *Female forms. Experiencing and understanding disability.* Buckingham: Open University Press.
Tomlinson, S. (1982). *A sociology of special education.* London: Routledge and Kegan Paul.
Tonkin, E. (1992). *Narrating our past. The social construction of oral history.* Cambridge: Cambridge University Press.
Usher, R. (1996). A critique of the neglected epistemological assumptions of educational research. In D. Scott & R. Usher (Eds.), *Understanding educational research* (pp. 9–32). London: Routledge.
Ware, L. (2007). A look at the way we look at disability. In S. Danforth & S. Gabel (Eds.), *Vital questions facing disability studies in education* (pp. 242–264). New York: Peter Lang.
World Health Organization. (2001). *International classification of functioning, disability and health* (ICF). Geneva: Author.
Yow, V. R. (1994). *Recording oral history.* California: Sage.
Zarb, G. (1992). On the road to Damascus: First steps towards changing the relations of disability research production. *Disability, Handicap and Society, 7*(2), 125–138.
Zarb, G. (1997). Researching disabling barriers. In C. Barnes & G. Mercer (Eds.), *Doing disability research* (pp. 49–66). Leeds: The Disability Press.

ILEKTRA SPANDAGOU

5. THE ELUSIVE SEARCH FOR INCLUSIVE EDUCATION IN A COMPARATIVE STUDY

INTRODUCTION

I write this chapter ten years after I completed my PhD study and almost 16 years since I first started my doctoral studies. In the not so far past of the middle 1990s, the urgency for timely completion was much less than my students and I as a supervisor currently experience. I was, therefore, able to take my time as a full-time student. I was in my mid twenties when I started, straight from finishing my Masters and with only one year of working in schools after my undergraduate degree. I am originally from Greece and moved to England for my postgraduate studies. I completed both my Masters and PhD at the University of Sheffield and during these years my experiences were about living in a different country as well as studying. I had no family responsibilities and for part of my doctoral studies I worked sporadically and in short-term jobs. It was only towards the end of my fieldwork and data collection that I worked full-time as a researcher for about 18 months. This job, which I still consider part of my training as a researcher, allowed me to develop my skills and to write, in my view, a more considered final thesis. However, I needed to resign from my position to actually complete the thesis, since I lacked the discipline to complete the writing-up in the evenings and weekends after long hours at work.

Overall, I was in what I considered then, but even more so now, a privileged position in terms of the practical aspects of financial security and time availability. Being in this privileged position did not mean of course that completing doctoral research was an easy undertaking or that life did not interfere with my project. The reason I provide this information is that who I was then defined the questions I asked, the way I asked them and my ability to search for answers. Looking back at my younger self, I fitted the profile of a young graduate student with years of experience of being a student and less experience in other roles. Engaging in a PhD was not simply an apprenticeship to being a researcher and potentially an academic, but also a process of personal maturation. In the following sections I will revisit that process by discussing how the study was conceptualized, the theoretical and methodological framework that informed my work and the implications of those decisions in the realization of the study and the writing-up of the thesis. Even though this chapter aims to describe some of the messiness of the research process, the division into sections and the linear discussion reinforces a sense of order. Perhaps

S. Symeonidou and K. Beauchamp-Pryor (Eds.), Purpose, Process and Future Direction of Disability Research, 59–72.

this presentation is unavoidable and after all this is the story of a PhD research project that was successfully completed. However, since I am still asking and struggling with the same questions and issues, this is an ongoing journey for me.

THE STARTING POINT

The title of my thesis was *Comparative and ethnographic research on inclusion: The case of English and Greek secondary education*. Despite the title's triteness, it stated what was important to me: to conduct a comparative study on inclusion. I started my study two years after the Salamanca Statement (UNESCO, 1994) and inclusion then was a new concept and in fact it did not have a working translation in Greek. By a working translation I mean a translation that could be considered as generally accepted. Even now a number of different and competing terms are used in Greek for the policies and practices that claim to promote inclusive education. A further difficulty was the translating and incorporating of the Greek inclusive discourse into the international inclusive discourse, since the lack of a working translation could potentially result in a power imbalance between languages. Simply put, what is described in one language as inclusion could dominate possible expressions of inclusion in a different language. Overall, I considered inclusion as a mystifying term due to its partial translation to my own language.

Inclusion was not the only new term that I was mystified by, but it was the most problematic for me as I was trying to grasp the difference between integration, which was the existing, dominant model of mainstream education for children categorized as having special educational needs at that period, and inclusion. Thus, integration was the known and inclusion was the unknown. The irony was that integration had been introduced to the Greek educational context in a very similar way, but over time it became an established discourse with influence in educational debates, policy and practice. I was suspicious of inclusion and the potential for inclusion to be imposed on the Greek educational system without consideration of the particular characteristics of this educational system as a form of intellectual and policymaking imperialism (Corbett, 1998). My suspicion was a valid one, but at the same time an expression of my naivety to critically engage in a historical perspective with the discourses that had influenced my educational standpoint.

For someone new to the field the term integration is often viewed now as having mainly historical relevance, which was not the case in the early 1990s. Saying that neither inclusion, nor integration for that matter, have a definition that is consensually accepted. The multiple definitions of inclusion mean that inclusion is a slippery term at a theoretical, policy and practice level. Looking for an example of inclusion that is representative of all possible definitions is, therefore, a futile exercise. In hindsight and as an aside, it can be argued that there is a perceived difference between inclusion and special education, with the latter being defined by distinctive knowledge and practices, in contrast to the value driven orientation of inclusion. Although for the most part inclusive education makes limited, if any, claims to new, specialized knowledge, it is not more valued driven than special education, or any other aspect of education.

Returning to the study, I was also fascinated by inclusion as a concept. My impression was that inclusion had the potential to open new ways of understanding education and move our thinking beyond special education to incorporate difference and plurality in schools, providing at the same time a critical insight to both special and general education. Of course, there were different ways of defining inclusion and the definition that I was aligning with did not view the presence of disabled children in mainstream settings as the ultimate goal, but rather promoted educational reform for all children (Barton, 1995). This was an understanding of inclusion that I was familiar with and I was able to relate it to the Greek educational debates, which at that time were still very much informed by the neo-marxist educational thinking of the 1970s and 1980s.

In summing up, my first reaction to inclusion was to perceive inclusion as the unknown (something I did not know) and alien (something I did not have experience of), although I was able to draw upon my personal experience (in terms of the struggle for a more equitable and democratic education in the Greek education system) to help me in approaching the concept. I started with the simplistic aim of finding a translation. However, whilst I realized that seeking a translation might facilitate the communication between the two languages and educational discourses and make inclusion a known term in Greece, the quest for a translation did not necessarily solve the issue of inclusion as an alien term. The question then was whether it was possible to have alternative understandings of inclusion, which could be applied in a number of contexts without leading to alien, imposed and monolithic/dominant representations in these contexts. The other side of this question was whether it was possible to have an understanding of inclusion that transcended localized definitions, and at the same time incorporated them.

In problematizing the above questions, I tried to check my own past experiences with my new knowledge and to reflect on how I constructed new knowledge based on my past experiences. I was doing what Okely called exploration of the 'abstractions contained in our anecdotes' (1996, p. 149) by connecting biography, history and society (Mills, 1971). At that stage, I also started to question the part of comparative research in which, more often than not, there was no information about what actually happened in the everyday world of schools and classrooms. However, my understanding of inclusion developed in a comparative framework. A framework which was comparative in two ways: inclusion was not viewed in isolation, but in relation to exclusion; and inclusion/exclusion were considered in the context where experiences took place. Whilst I am aware that my approach might appear to be self-indulgent, I used this process not only as a constant exercise in self-reflection and as a questioning of my own understanding of concepts, but also as a methodological tool during fieldwork in both countries. Gordon, Holland and Lahelma argued that 'in memory work shared cultural codes can be tapped' (2000, p. 55) and perhaps this is part of what I was trying to achieve. Finally, the process of moving between

61

present and past, educational systems, schools, and the literature influenced the way I understood theorizing and researching.

For me this type of research was seen as deeply personal and political. I have to admit that for most of the time of engaging with my research project I did not perceive the findings as having the potential of instigating change and in some respects I was self-indulgent because I viewed the research in terms of my own research 'obsessions' and personal development and knowledge. On the one hand my position was liberating, because my personal journey became my guiding compass. On the other hand, my approach defined to large extent the possibilities of what my study was about.

In the next section, I reflect in terms of what my study was, and was not, about. The main assumptions which informed my approach are detailed: assumptions which defined and underpinned what was important, but at the same time tacitly indicate aspects that were ignored or overlooked.

THE CONCEPTUALIZATION OF THE STUDY

My research was about inclusion and exclusion in schools. Inclusion and exclusion were defined in relation to difference and in turn difference was understood as encompassing disability, gender, race, class, religion and culture amongst others. Difference was also defined as socially constructed, as the actual and perceived attributes and characteristics of individuals and groups that affect, and in cases determine, how individuals and groups are perceived in relation to assumed normality.

Thus, the aim of the study was to explore how structures, practices, attitudes and perceptions were defined and interpreted as inclusive/exclusive by the participants in educational settings (secondary schools in England and Greece) and how these interpretations were influenced by, and in their turn influenced, the socioeconomic, political and cultural context in which they took place. In this respect, difference was perceived as both real and contested. Difference is real because it constitutes part of the struggle for participation and inclusion, and contested because what difference means can change as part of this struggle.

In addition, the word dialogue was used in order to describe the research relations between the two units of comparison (England and Greece). These research relations did not try to establish which system was 'better' as far as inclusion was concerned. Neither did they attempt to define good practice in an abstract way, which did not take into account the context, the purposes and the structural characteristics of each educational system. The aim of this dialogue was to find out whether the obvious similarities and differences between the two educational systems were really so obvious and to explore their influence in the construction of inclusion in each context. A number of assumptions, which are presented in the rest of this section, informed this approach.

The main assumption underlining the use of similarities and differences was that, as Tomlinson (1982) argued, special education has the ideological function to control the smooth working of general education, which is unable or unwilling to educate a large part of the school population. Special education is only one of the ways in which children are differentiated or selected in education. These ways of selection are internal characteristics of general education and they can be found in the organization of schools, teaching methods, curriculum, and processes of assessment and examination (Apple, 1996). The exclusive practices of general education and how these practices function and are legitimated in a given educational system (Slee, 1998) are central in order to explore the relationship between general and special education and the influence that this relationship has on the conceptualization of inclusion. The comparative implication of this is that different educational systems, because of the specific objectives that they have in the sociopolitical, economic and cultural contexts in which they exist, may have different ways of selecting and excluding students, as well as of including them.

Secondly, the discourse of needs was central in understanding the relationship between special and general education (Barton & Oliver, 1992). How needs are understood influences the provision made for these needs as well as which groups are defined as having (special) needs and by whom and where these needs are catered for. The social model of disability challenges the perception that the needs of children are internal, individual characteristics, which leads to the notion that needs are constructed and defined by the social environment (Barnes, 1997; Morris, 1993; Oliver, 1990; 1996; 2009; Oliver & Barnes, 2012). At a comparative level, different educational systems not only respond in different ways to needs and allocate them accordingly in general and special education, but also they may recognize different needs.

A discourse of needs in which one tries to answer the question of how and why needs are constructed in general education cannot avoid examining the notions of knowledge/ability and discipline/behavior. What is considered as normal in schools and how students are compared and categorized according to their individual characteristics and the expectations of teachers, are linked to the creation of dichotomies (Slee, 1993) such as normal/pathological, good/bad, appropriate/ inappropriate. The concept of needs is also connected to the vested interests of professionals who are responsible for identifying, assessing and providing for these needs, and of other involved groups such as parents and the disabled people's movement (Fulcher, 1989). The relationship amongst all these groups and their power positions has also a comparative dimension since the provision made by different systems and the participation of different groups in policymaking may differ as well.

Thirdly, the relationship between educational systems and the wider context not only affects general and special education, but also the position of these contexts at an international level. The globalization of education, the influence of multilateral organizations such as United Nations Educational, Scientific and Cultural Organization (UNESCO), Organization for Economic Co-operation and Development (OECD) and European Union (EU), and international discourses of education are factors that are involved in policymaking. The process of policy initiation, implementation and negotiation and the distinction between written, stated and enacted policy (Fulcher, 1989) was another comparative dimension. Policy and practice do not happen in isolation within the confines of a nation state. The educational reforms in England and Greece during the period covered by this study, and also in the last few years defined by the global financial crisis, have been promoted and justified by discourses both international and specific to each country. In examining these external influences I sought to identify why different systems have similar developments and to challenge the assumption that these developments are natural.

Finally, the values associated with inclusion determine the way that inclusion can be achieved and can be researched. These values are not always stated and inclusion may be presented as free from values and assumptions, and more as a technical issue rather than as a theoretical one. Even the fundamental right to a common education for all students cannot be seen as having an unquestionable validity but rather as being an ideological position which needs to substantiate its validity and meaning in the democratic discourse of education. In this context, the research study had three aims:

- To explore the concepts of inclusion/exclusion and their relationship to changing social identities in the context of a citizenship/democracy discourse.
- To explore the concepts of inclusion/exclusion in relation to changes in the organization of schooling.
- To examine the concepts of inclusion/exclusion in a cross-national context.

From these aims a number of research questions concerning inclusion/exclusion were asked:

- For what reasons are inclusive practices introduced and how are these reasons connected to different discourses of needs and schooling?
- With which groups of students are inclusive practices concerned and what are the objectives in relation to these groups and the educational system in general?
- What are the exclusive practices that take place in the same context as inclusive practices?
- Does any conflict occur between inclusive and exclusive practices and for what reasons?
- Is the process of inclusion met by resistance and if yes, for what reasons and by which groups?

To sum up, two main assumptions were formulated for defining inclusion/exclusion in this study. Firstly, inclusion/exclusion was considered as a value/ideological concept. The phenomenon, processes and practices of inclusion/exclusion, took place in different educational and societal contexts, and related to how the concept of inclusion/exclusion was defined by all the participants involved. Secondly, inclusion as a discourse was viewed as part of a democratic/citizenship discourse in education. Inclusion/exclusion could then be explored in contexts where the term inclusion was not used, and referenced to general education as much as to special education.

To some extent, special and general education as a clear dichotomy was questioned by the inclusive discourse. This conceptualization started forming before the actual fieldwork and informed the methodology of the study, but it was during fieldwork and the process of writing-up the thesis that this conceptualization took its final form. The next section discusses the methodology of the research and presents some aspects of the messiness of the process of data collection.

THE MESSINNESS OF THE RESEARCH PROCESS

Reflecting back to the initial conceptualization of the study, a comparative ethnographic approach was selected because it had the potential to produce detailed information about what inclusion is and how it is defined in the two contexts and in a way that (hopefully) could lead to 'sound' comparisons. However, at that time I was unsure whether I was able to make sound comparisons. One reason for my lack of confidence was the fact that the conceptualization of inclusion presented in the previous section, was not based on the assumption of an explicit conceptual equivalence. There is a degree of theoretical equivalence in so far as the underlying meaning of inclusion, as struggle for participation and citizenship, is similar in different contexts. However, the expression of this struggle can take different forms in different contexts. This conceptualization then is methodologically problematic since it does not focus the topic on specific expressions of inclusion, nor does it give indications of what exactly inclusion is and where it can be found and researched.

Whilst I was comfortable with this theoretical messiness, I was looking for order in the research process. Thus, I attempted to design my study with a degree of methodological/sampling equivalence. Taking this approach meant that the ethnographic studies in the two countries would have followed the methodological tradition of school ethnography with the ultimate aim to produce comparable data. The quest for methodological equivalence proved problematic from the start. The actual complexities of the fieldwork affected how the study developed. My personal decision was to avoid, as far as possible, using labels of disability and of difference in general in selecting schools and individuals to participate in the research. Thus the reality of the English school (where specific policies and practices for students categorized as having special needs and for other groups were present) and the Greek school (where a common provision was perceived as appropriate and adequate for the majority of students) were seen as representative and meaningful in their respective contexts. I decided hence to avoid finding comparable schools with similar policies because it would have meant that in each context such schools would have been exceptional.

Adopting this approach did not mean a complete lack of sampling decisions. For example, all schools were urban schools and in the English school the three years of the lower school were selected as corresponding to the three years of the Greek compulsory secondary education. However, the actual data collection was a period with ups and downs and many changes. Any hope for similar research experiences in the two contexts soon vanished and managing the disappointment and uncertainty involved was part of the process of learning to be a researcher. A short description of the different stages of data collection is provided aiming also to give an indication of how far from two comparable stages of data collection the actual fieldwork was.

English School

Access to the school had been arranged at the end of the previous year. In the English school I stayed for nine months (September 1997 to the beginning of June 1998) for three days a week. One year form was selected from each year of the lower school as the main sample of the research. All of the year forms included a number of students with statements of special educational needs and support staff were present in most of the lessons. In the subjects where these year forms were in ability groups, I observed the lower ability class. I observed a variety of subjects and I was also acting as a volunteer teaching assistant.

The 88 students from the three year forms (covering the three years of the lower school) constituted the main sample of the research, but the number of students observed on a regular basis was around 160 from the 750 students at the school. Interviews were conducted with 59 of the 88 students from the three year forms and 19 members of staff. Staff members included: the head teacher, special needs co-ordinator, two teaching members of the special needs education department, five teaching assistants, and ten subject teachers (including one form tutor and two members of the senior management team). Finally, a number of documents were examined about the organization of the school, and student files from the special needs department and records concerned with discipline were reviewed.

First Greek School

Arrangements for access started in May 1998 by submitting an application to receive permission to conduct research. However, when I returned to Greece in September 1998, I found out that the application was not processed because it was assessed as incomplete and no one had contacted me asking for corrections. A second application was submitted in September with a two month expected processing time. In October, an outbreak of student activism, due to proposed changes in education by the Government, resulted in students closing the schools. By Christmas, approximately 2,000 out of the 3,534 secondary schools in Greece were closed. Schools started opening again after the Christmas period and I received official permission to conduct research in February 1999, when the unrest was over. In the meantime, I participated in numerous student demonstrations and collected materials from student publications and mainstream media about the student movement. An overview and discussion of student unrest was later incorporated into the thesis. The disruption of the school year meant that a long stay in a school was impossible. Following the disruption schools were required to operate longer hours and/or at the weekends to compensate for the missed teaching hours.

The research in the school started in March and I went to the school for 15 days up to June. Similar to the English school, three year forms were selected (one from each year) and one observation was conducted in each year form during which I presented the research project to the students and provided them with the letters of consent. Interviews were conducted with 22 students. The year forms were selected based on the opinions of one teacher and the head teacher who considered the students to be 'challenging'. No documents were examined since the Ministry of Education did not give me access to the student files. During the fieldwork at the school, I felt that I was simply collecting data for the sake of collecting data and that I had lost a clear direction for the study. The long waiting period and the upset to all my expectations affected my motivation. I stopped the fieldwork and returned to England contemplating the abandonment of the comparative dimension of the research. Later, I decided to return and collect some further data from a second school in Greece, aiming however for a qualitative case study, rather than a longer ethnographic fieldwork.

Second Greek School

Access was arranged from November 1999 until the beginning of January 2000 and the fieldwork took place in February 2000. Three year forms were selected, one from each year, and 37 interviews were conducted with students over four days. The selection of the year forms was almost arbitrary: one year form was selected based upon the opinion of the head teacher and another teacher who thought the form was 'difficult'; and the other two forms were selected as typical of the school. A questionnaire was completed by 19 of the 29 teachers.

Analytical Themes

It is difficult even now to describe how disappointed I was by my failure to conduct two comparable ethnographic fieldworks in the two countries. It took me a while to be able to approach the experience with some analytical clarity. When I did start analysing the material from the three schools, two theoretical, methodological and analytical themes emerged. I used these themes to bridge the theoretical framework and the reality of research by once more questioning my assumptions. A process which was a core part of the analysis.

The first theme was of *closed/open spaces and ownership*. Inclusion/exclusion may be perceived as the right to participate in specific settings, at the same time as the right of owning/having a say about these settings. Inclusion then is not a passive right that is given to individuals and groups. Arranging access for research in Greece is an example of a methodological application. Access is controlled centrally and involves a procedure starting from the top (Ministry of Education) and ending at the school.

The system as a whole gave the impression of a closed one where decision-making/ ownership comes from above. However, the school, the head teacher or the teachers as a group or individuals, may accept (or not), or give their own interpretation to the central decision, and can therefore choose whether to close and open the school to the researcher. At an analytical level, the closure of schools by the students was an example of change of ownership of school space and reversal of control. In this particular case ownership was connected explicitly to notions of citizenship.

The second theme was about *knowledge construction*. At a methodological level, while in Greece I experienced great difficulties to obtaining access to schools, I had felt secure in my knowledge of the system and culture (of being an insider). At the English school I had the opposite experience, where developing an understanding of the context took time. Initially, I experienced a difficultly in describing events: for example, a lesson without comparison or starting from my own experience. As Burgess argued, 'of all social institutions, schools are highly familiar settings' (1984, p. 26), but familiarity does not necessarily constitute understanding. The differences I identified in lesson structure, teaching and learning methods and pedagogy were crucial in identifying what inclusion was in the two educational systems and whether or not inclusion was restricted by such differences. Moreover, knowledge construction related at an analytical level to notions of competence/incompetence, including what constitutes a competent researcher and in constructions of special education needs, as I repeatedly found in the data. The way that these two themes brought together theory, methodology and analysis allowed me to come to terms with what can be seen as the necessity of research messiness. Of course this does not mean that I would not have preferred the data collection process to be more straightforward.

The next section discusses another aspect of the study which I struggled with: the relationship of my work with the social model of disability.

THE RESEARCH PROJECT AND THE SOCIAL MODEL OF DISABILITY

Whilst my study was informed by the social model of disability, I did not adopt a participatory or emancipatory approach to research. Barnes argued that 'there is no independent haven or middle ground when researching oppression; academics and researchers can only be with the oppressors or with the oppressed' (1996, p. 110). In this respect, the aim of a research project needs to be explicitly political promoting the struggle of disabled people for social change. Two models of research are found within this type of research: participatory and emancipatory. Participatory research aims to challenge social divisions and the power relationship of researcher-researched, and give the participants of the research a voice. Participatory research is considered as 'compatible with the social model of disability but not dependent on it' (Finkelstein, 1999, p. 863) and not as changing the social and material relations of research (which is the ultimate role and aim of emancipatory research). In emancipatory research the researcher devolves his/her control to disabled people throughout the research process, including the stages of research design, collection of data, analysis and dissemination. As Stone and Priestley argued, the emancipatory model 'requires full ownership of the means of research production – ownership by the research participants, not the researcher' (1996, p. 709).

My study was not designed as an emancipatory study. None of the students participating in the research project were involved in the design of the study in an explicit way. Thus, the issues explored, may or may not have been important for the students. Their school lives did not change as a result of the research, and generally students had no control over the study. The same, more or less, applied to the teachers participating in the research (for instance, only two people at the English school participated in the process of designing the interview questions and in Greece involvement happened at the level of the Ministry of Education).

Furthermore, disability was not the main focus of my research. The majority of the participants were young people. Participants included boys and girls, some of whom were labeled as having special educational needs, some as disabled, and some were from different ethnic and religious backgrounds. These young people belonged to different social classes according to the classifications used in the countries where the research took place. In addition, interpretations of gender, class, race, ability, religion, and culture in the two contexts differed. The views and interpretations of these young people about their school experiences were, therefore, characterized by diversity.

The research study was conducted by me, an adult, able-bodied, middle class, Greek woman, and in some cases my experiences and interpretations of education were different from those of the participants of the study. In writing-up the final thesis, I debated whether to disclose my own experiences as a student in the Greek educational system, including my experiences of discrimination, which were not related to disability, but to the fact that I was not registered as having a religion in a setting where almost all participants were identified with the same religion. I chose not to do so, I felt then and I am still of the same view, that any personal attributes of difference did not mean any greater level of understanding of the diverse experiences of the participants in the study. However, being a woman in my mid twenties was a very visible personal characteristic. Looking back, I believe that being a young woman made it easier for me to be accepted at the schools, since I looked like a university undergraduate student and was quite often assumed to be by most adult participants. Perhaps not being seen as a researcher gave me access to information and situations that I would not have gained otherwise.

The above points raised four methodological questions:

– What gave me the right to conduct research with these young people?
– To what extent was I able to understand their diverse experiences?
– What gave me the right to make claims about their interpretations of inclusion/ exclusion?
– Was it possible to construct a common political agenda from these diverse experiences?

These questions are different from the ones asked in an emancipatory study. My questions were mainly concerned with my political and moral obligation as the researcher and the relevance of the research to the researched context. From this position, it is assumed that the researcher more or less owns the research since he/she is the one taking most of the decisions about the study.

As discussed earlier, the initial theoretical and methodological question was whether it was possible to make a comparison without assuming that one state of affairs (in this case an educational system) was better. I do not know whether this theoretical question was important for disabled students, minority students, or any other students in the schools, and whether answering it would have made any difference to their lives. I consider, however, my question to be a political one, questioning the ways that success and failure, discrimination and oppression, and ultimately possibilities for change, are constrained by the values and assumptions that underpin comparisons within and outside educational systems.

CONCLUSION

Through the years I have been asked many times about my PhD topic. In response I explain that my research project was a comparative study of inclusion in England and Greek secondary schools. A common follow-up question is: Which of the two systems does inclusion better? This is a question that I find difficult to answer and usually I give an evasive, general answer. It is important to note, that none of the participants in my study described education and schooling as totally inclusive or exclusive (although for some of the participants education has to be inclusive in principle), but rather participants described education as conditionally inclusive or exclusive. I tried to capture this complexity in the final text of the thesis.

The final analysis and writing-up processes were defined by the urgency of submitting on time, after exhausting a number of extensions and testing the endless goodwill of my supervisor. I still consider the analytical framework of my study relevant to the field of inclusive education and in general, I do not feel embarrassed if required to read again the final text. However, there are aspects of the analysis and of the thesis that I wish I had gained more experience of before completion, and issues which I would welcome the opportunity to revisit. Two questions that I would have liked the opportunity to explore further are:

– In what ways students in schools relate their experiences of inclusion and exclusion to the broader socioeconomic, political and cultural context and how these experiences affect their construction of notions of citizenship?
– Can comparative research inform a pedagogy that promotes inclusion?

I do not believe that my findings had much of an impact. Whilst I have used ideas and some extracts in writings (for example, Armstrong, Armstrong & Spandagou, 2010), I have not published specifically from my research until now. I feel ambivalent about this outcome because such limited dissemination does not acknowledge the sharing of experiences, views, and time of the participants. I am currently involved in the supervision of comparative research studies by doctoral students and it is a fulfilling experience to work on similar issues with them. The expectation of timely completion, the requirements of ethics approval in different contexts, the costs of conducting fieldwork in different countries are practical issues that we discuss from the early stages of the study. As a supervisor I aim for my students to avoid some of the pitfalls that I have experienced. However, I am aware that this is their journey and it is for them to steer their research in the direction they choose.

Finally, I wrote this chapter referring to my research and my decisions. However, the influence of my supervisor, Derrick Armstrong, was invaluable. I take responsibility for the limitations of the study and the final text, but I am fully aware that I would not have been able to complete the research project without the support of my supervisor. His support was practical, as well as intellectual, and as a novice researcher I found both types of support essential. I was also fortunate to be in a faculty which was intellectually stimulating and where inclusive education was a core research interest. My research interests were nurtured in an environment which provided a safety net for me to take risks in pursuing my research study.

REFERENCES

Apple, M. (1996). *Cultural politics in education*. New York: Teachers College Press.

Armstrong, A. C., Armstrong, D., & Spandagou, I. (2010). *Inclusive education: International policy & practice*. London: Sage.

Barnes, C. (1996). Disability and the myth of the independent researcher. *Disability and Society, 11*(1), 107–110.

Barnes, C. (1997). A legacy of oppression: A history of disability in western culture. In L. Barton & M. Oliver (Eds.), *Disabilities studies: Past, present and future* (pp. 3–24). Leeds: The Disability Press.

Barton, L. (1995). The politics of education for all. *Support for Learning, 10*(4), 156–160.

Barton, L., & Oliver, M. (1992). Special needs; Personal trouble or public issue. In M. Arnot & L. Barton (Eds.), *Voicing concerns: Sociological perspectives on contemporary education reforms* (pp. 66–87). Wallingford: Triangle Books.

Burgess, R. (1984). *In the field: An introduction to field research*. London: Routledge.

Corbett, J. (1998). *Special educational needs in the twentieth century: A cultural analysis*. London: Cassell.

Finkelstein, V. (1999). *Doing disability research* [Book Review]. *Disability and Society, 14*(6), 859–878.

Fulcher, G. (1989). *Disabling policies? A comparative approach to educational policy and disability*. London: The Falmer Press.

Gordon, T., Holland, J., & Lahelma, E. (2000). *Making spaces: Citizenship and difference in schools*. London: MacMillan.

Mills, C. W. (1971). *The sociological imagination* (2nd ed.). New York: Penguin Books.

Morris, J. (1993). Gender and disability. In J. Swain, V. Finkelstein, S. French & M. Oliver (Eds.), *Disabling barriers – enabling environments* (pp. 85–92). London: Sage.

Okely, J. (1996). *Own or other culture*. London: Routledge.

Oliver, M. (1990). *The politics of disablement*. London: Macmillan.

Oliver, M. (1996). *Understanding disability: From theory to practice*. London: Macmillan.

Oliver, M. (2009). *Understanding disability: From theory to practice* (2nd ed.). Basingstoke: Palgrave Macmillan.

Oliver, M., & Barnes, C. (2012). *The new politics of disablement*. Basingstoke: Palgrave. Macmillan.

Slee, R. (1993). The politics of integration – New sites for old practices? *Disability, Handicap and Society, 8*(4), 351–360.

Slee, R. (1998). The politics of theorising special education. In C. Clark, A. Dyson & A. Millward (Eds.), *Theorising special education* (pp. 126–136). London: Routledge.

Stone, E., & Priestley, M. (1996). Parasites, pawns and partners: Disability research and the role of non-disabled researchers. *International Journal of Sociology, 47*(4), 619–716.

Tomlinson, S. (1982). *Sociology of special education*. London: Routledge and Kegan Paul.

UNESCO. (1994). *The Salamanca statement and framework on special needs education*. Paris: UNESCO.

ELENI GAVRIELIDOU-TSIELEPI

6. RESEARCH IN POLICYMAKING IN EDUCATION: IS THERE A PLACE FOR THE SOCIAL MODEL?

INTRODUCTION

When I was asked to write about my personal journey through my PhD research project, I initially anticipated this as an easy task. I assumed that this long, agonizing and full of crossroads trip was well committed to memory as were the decisions made easy to explain. This was not to be the case. Following unsuccessful attempts to trace back important methodological and other dilemmas, I recalled the suggestion of Len Barton, one of my mentors, who advised me to record my thoughts, difficulties and anxieties in a reflective research diary. Initially, I did not anticipate the relevance of this task to the research project. However, in the first of a series of diaries that I started writing soon after his recommendation, I found my unconditional devotion to the principles of the social model and an analytical and well thought, as I believed, research plan. Being born and raised in Cyprus, a country which still subscribes to the medical model of disability and the principles of charity and philanthropy, I had to look deeper to recall my first encounter with the social model and to record its influence in personal thinking.

I remember being introduced to the principles of the social model as a student at the University of Cyprus between 1995 and 1999 where I was studying to become a pre-primary school teacher. In the compulsory course for the 'Introduction to Special Education' we had a particularly critical discussion about the social practices that promote the disablement of impaired citizens. We were asked to closely observe the events organized, the language used and the practices of everyday life, in order to briefly express our understandings regarding the issue discussed. Not surprisingly, I was part of the great majority of students who viewed through positive spectacles, the various philanthropic events. The stepping up of private initiative in areas the state failed to finance (for example the integration of children classified as having 'special needs' within the mainstream setting) was considered at the time as an additional force towards the realization of disabled citizens human rights. Nobody was meant to comment on our views and we were asked instead to put aside our writing whilst we read about the social model and the principles of inclusive education. Upon my return to the initial piece of writing (at the end of the term), having been deeply influenced by Michael Oliver (whose writing I found very instructive and informative), and Len Barton (whom I was fortunate to listen to when he delivered a passionate lecture as a guest lecturer during one

S. Symeonidou and K. Beauchamp-Pryor (Eds.), Purpose, Process and Future Direction of Disability Research, 73–88.

of our sessions), I found myself being on the opposing side of the medical model (again with the majority of students). I was suddenly disturbed with the continual organization of philanthropic events, the sole focus on money collection and the constant use of sensational narratives such as 'unfortunate people with problems', 'suffering fellowmen', 'victims of fate' or 'fighters of life'. Suddenly I considered these terms as highlighting the deeply embedded perception that disability equals personal tragedy (Oliver, 1990; Oliver & Barnes, 2012). I began to perceive various charity events in a very different light. I noted the continuous portrayal of disabled people as extraordinary and the emphasis on how they were different from the rest because they had 'special needs'. The advertisements to raise money frequently used images of disabled people in a dramatic way and were always accompanied by the appropriate background music that produced feelings of sadness and pity.

This turning point experience intrigued me and was pivotal in the selecting of inclusive education as the specialization path of my bachelor degree, and later on in deciding to undertake a masters course at the University of Bristol in the education of children categorized as having 'special educational needs'. My underlying motive was to make a difference, to provide an alternative perspective through more informed teaching and to be one of the first pre-primary school teachers to work in this field, which was to be substantially altered as a result of the official implementation of the new law for the integration of children classified as having 'special needs' in the mainstream school (Republic of Cyprus, 1999) in 2001, the second year of my appointment in the local mainstream schools. During this period of my professional life, I lay engulfed in a substantially differentiated reality. As a pre-primary school teacher I was disappointed in the perceived inability of the educational system to promote a more inclusive educational setting. This initiated a deeper investigation of certain understandings and the pursuit of further research.

The following section attempts to critically reflect on the choices made, the dilemmas encountered and the overall process of conducting a PhD research project, as well as the ways in which the ideas and principles of the social model determined the decisions I made. An emphasis is placed on the personal experience and the ways in which preconceived ideas and understandings were important throughout my research journey. In addition, the work of Fulcher (1999) and the notions of power and micro-politics determined the lenses through which the research questions were explored.

ARRIVING AT RESEARCHING POLICY ISSUES

My initial appointment as a pre-primary school teacher was at a single-placed school. This meant that I was the only teacher at the school and my duties entailed teaching all students enrolled plus exercising the duties normally assigned to the principal. A unique opportunity existed to put in to practice my knowledge and to embark on the dream of bringing about change in everyday practice: the first step being this one small school. The initial excitement was soon compromised with the realities of everyday practice. Despite the official implementation of *The 1999 Education Act for the Education of Children with Special Needs* (Republic of Cyprus, 1999), which introduced the policy of integration and the notion of the 'least restrictive environment', everyday practice was substantially different. The new law, regardless of establishing the right of all children to be educated in the mainstream school, did not challenge the injustices against disabled children. The emphasis on 'needs' detracted from a proper consideration of rights, which was central to the notion of inclusion. On the contrary, the legal framework focused on the establishment of the procedures for diagnosis, individual separate support and the clarification of the role of professionals. My realization concerning the gap between policy and everyday practice, ultimately led to the research which forms the basis for the present chapter.

My initial attempt to explore policymaking began with the false understanding of policy being solely the legal framework which provides the guidelines for action: guidelines that practitioners, such as myself, implement without the power to question or alter. Therefore change in policy would equal change in practice. Consequently, the failure of the new law in Cyprus to bring about change in everyday practice, apart from the technicalities of assessment and the labeling of children, raised queries and concerns over what I perceived as omissions and misinterpretations of the provisions of the law.

Following submission of the above apprehensions in the form of a PhD research proposal in 2003 to the Institute of Education, University of London, one of the first tasks I was asked to undertake was to read Fulcher's (1999) work. Her approach to policy provided a context within which these understandings could be explored, overthrowing my initial interpretation of policymaking. Fulcher (1999) argues that policy is not a top-down process; it is not made by government and handed down ready-made to be implemented. Policy is a product of negotiations and struggles over vested interests and ideology and is made at all levels, official (parliamentary meetings) and unofficial (meetings attended by teachers, social gatherings of teachers or parents, and decisions reached by teachers within the classroom), with the participation of a number of actors. Policy is seen as an ongoing process rather than as the final product (Ozga, 2000) and is understood as referring to something which is different from, and more than, decisions taken by political leaders. Therefore policy is not solely the governmental mandates or the legal frameworks (written policy) but also the practices, discussions and decisions made concerning daily actions (enacted policy). The important idea is that policy is not one or the other, but both. They are 'implicit in each other' (Ball, 1994). Although educational policy:

Involves exercise of governmental authority, [...] government officials and authority figures are not the only people involved, nor are they necessarily the leading players. (Colebatch, 1998, p. 40)

This provided a context in which my personal experience could be understood and the constant contradictions between written and enacted policy could be explored.

My initial exploration of policymaking literature gave way to more questions: if policy constituted a product of negotiations and struggles over vested interests and ideology, how could a legal framework in Cyprus promote, as is proclaimed, the human rights of all children, a principle which was understood as closely associated with the social model of disability? In addition, who took part in the negotiations for this legal framework, how did they manage to influence the making of policy and what were their vested interests that determined the outcome of policy discussions? In an attempt to search deeper I began browsing the Greek literature hoping to find something more that the 'traditional history' (Foucault & Rabinow, 1994) of the education system and a more detailed account on the development of policy. Following weeks of unsuccessful searching I found myself in a deadlock. But then, at one of my meetings with Felicity Armstrong (my other mentor in this research project), I was directed to a presentation of a book by Gary McCulloch (2004) related to documentary research in education. Initially, I felt that this research book was irrelevant to my project. However, in reading the first few pages of the book I began to find common ground between my research and the author. Historical research does not only refer to past and forgotten accounts, but it constitutes an important means of understanding and addressing contemporary concerns (McCulloch, 2004). Soon, I realized that a historical background research was able to provide indicative material concerning the beliefs and the culture underpinning the 'making' of the law and those who participated in the decision-making, and how they influenced the outcome of the discussions. In addition, it was valuable in the exploration of the ways in which certain notions become the practice of today and are rationalized as 'common sense' (Bogdan & Biklen, 1992) (for example, the belief that children classified as having 'special needs' belong to a separate education system or that philanthropy is the means through which to provide for disabled people). Indeed historical research was helpful in illustrating how the 'taken for granted' assumptions and debates of the contemporary education system had developed over time. This historical enquiry had an additional use in my research: it enabled me to understand the origins of recent problems, it empowered me to ask questions about the present and investigate contemporary debates with increased awareness. With this in mind, I primarily searched for documentary evidence from the files of the Ministry of Education and Culture (MOEC). No other source of evidence could offer this information regarding the political decisions of the government, the actions or the inactions of the MOEC and the long term discussions for policy formulation in Cyprus. The analysis of the documents and records of the MOEC allowed for a deeper insight into the interests involved in the policymaking procedure, while the minutes and the correspondence between the MOEC and various other policy arenas enabled me to peep behind the curtain.

The historical insight provided by the documentary work was only the beginning of an attempt to shed light on contemporary policy concerns related to the ideology in which the current policy was embedded, the role of policy actors in the discussions for developing it and the ways they managed to influence the process. The powerlessness of disabled people to make their voices heard, even when they were actually participating in the process, was evident. At the same time the discourse of professionalism pervaded both the policy discussions recorded in documentary evidence and the text of the law. Documents and newspaper articles supported the argument that the dislodge of the medical model of disability was not an easily accomplished task. In fact, newspaper articles, which allowed me to go as far back as 1879, enabled the exploration of the construction of certain ideas and understandings which still prevail in policymaking. The continuous and determinate role of the Church during the long periods of the Turkish occupation (1571–1878) and the British administration (1878–1959) in Cyprus directed education under a more religious focus and substantially informed educational developments and responses to disability. In accordance with the long absence of a Cypriot government, Church established charity and philanthropy as the arenas for providing for the unfortunate fellowmen, while segregation and medicalization of disability gradually established themselves as the norm, something that is visible up until today (Symeonidou, 2009).

One of my biggest struggles during this journey was the reconstruction of my own personal understandings: how was it possible that the written or official policy did not have the power to determine everyday practice or that the legal framework did not constitute the end of policy discussions? Documentary research also facilitated this conflict of personal understandings and literature by providing solid examples of this 'inconsistency' between written and enacted policy. Such examples arose from the context of Cyprus and they matched with both the historical accounts that I studied in detail during my undergraduate studies (for example, the troubled attempts to integrate children classified as having 'special needs' in mainstream schools at the beginning of the 1980s) and with my personal experience as a teacher (for example, different schools in their attempt to implement a common legal framework resulted in a substantially differentiated everyday reality). Policy was interpreted and reinterpreted in various ways by different participants according to their understandings, interests and beliefs, without this implying the existence of a correct or expected interpretation.

My realization that the formulation of the legal framework did not conclude policy discussion emphasized the need to continue the project but under a differentiated context: that of policy implementation. This is not to argue that there is a clear distinction between policymaking and policy implementation but to emphasize the change of research methods in order to explore policy as everyday practice. The research questions remained concerned with the policy actors who managed to influence the policymaking procedure, the hidden power struggles amongst them and the strategies they employed to achieve their ends. The major challenge discussed in the section that follows was the way in which the research methods were combined in an attempt to provide an in-depth and critical discussion concerning the unique development of history in the context of Cyprus.

THEORETICAL AND METHODOLOGICAL FRAMEWORK: THE MEANS TO EXPLORE THE RESEARCH QUESTIONS

Policy is an ongoing process to be investigated in differentiated settings: notably the discussion of formulation in the form of documents and the implementation of policy in the educational settings. The contribution of a variety of actors, official and unofficial, was inevitable. Realizing all these accentuated the necessity for the use of a combination of research methods. This attempted not to provide an objective policy account but to give voice to differentiated perceptions of events and simply provide different angles for possible interpretations. The decisions made in constructing the methodological framework that would facilitate the exploration of the policymaking procedure constituted both the most troublesome part of this journey and the most challenging step towards researching policy in the continuity of its development.

Although both phases of the research were directly related to policymaking and the actors who influenced this process, I was concerned that I was in fact dealing with substantially different material, which consequently demanded a different methodological framework. The initial phase, that of historical/documentary research, was conducted through the interpretation and combination of documents and newspaper articles, while the second phase was carried out in schools and was concerned with the everyday practices (enacted policy) and the implementation and reinterpretation of the legal framework. In an attempt to select the most appropriate research methods, I ended up in what Levi-Strauss (in Armstrong, 2003) calls a bricoleur, a researcher who draws on different research methods and techniques in an attempt to create an appropriate research practice for the most effective exploration of the research questions. This allowed me to combine strategies and methods in the way I considered necessary. In addition, due to the fact that the research practices were not set in advance, I had the flexibility to piece together components of a variety of qualitative methods. Multiplicity of approaches was helpful in dealing with such a difficult and complex issue as policy research. As a bricoleur, I was required to undertake a number of different responsibilities such as interviewing, observing and interpreting. I felt that the deficiencies that flow from one research method could be tackled by the use of a combination of different approaches something which provided an additional cross validation of the research data. An example of cross validation derived from the combination of observation and interviews. The observation data recorded and the possible interpretations discussed, provided my personal understandings of policy actors actions and interests. The use of interviews proved appropriate to discuss in-depth understandings and facilitated either the validation of my initial interpretations or the provisions of alternative perspectives.

It is important to acknowledge that the product of this work, the bricolage, was influenced by my personal understanding of events. As an increasing supporter of the social model, my quest was to identify the socially created characteristics of practices or language that create disability on top of a person's impairment. The historical research, always running parallel to the personal experience, helped focus the understanding of those social and cultural characteristics of the Cypriot society which in turn allowed the maintaining of the ideology of intrinsic 'needs'. Practices, such as the identification of 'needs' and the consequent labeling of the person were understood as contributing to the construction of disability as an intrinsic deficit and justified maintaining a differentiated educational setting solely for 'these' students and the growing numbers of professionals who 'helped' respond to diversity. For the theoretical framework of the project, I adopted a sociopolitical approach in which disability was understood as directly relating to the way we treated people, our attitudes and the opportunities we permitted them to have (Barton, 1986), and therefore we could eschew labeling, categorization and segregated education. Instead of attributing the child's difficulties to internal factors, my prime focus during both phases of research rested on the disabling impacts of society and the barriers and constraints of the education system (Drake, 1999). As I will discuss later on, personal experience constituted an essential part of my journey, even in the phase of data collection, and the final product, the bricolage, constituted a reflective creation that represented my images, understandings and interpretations of policy. This was to emphasize that the notion of the 'objective' truth was rejected (Armstrong, 2003). The contribution of the multiplicity of the research methods in the present research relied on the different pictures or interpretations of data that were allowed to emerge.

Personal experience, knowledge and understandings were also of importance in an attempt to select and interpret documents from the files of the MOEC. My own social, political and religious background provided inevitable guidance in understanding the context of each document and of the potential bias or interests (professional or personal) of the author (McCulloch, 2004). In an attempt to read between the lines, it was important to identify the historical background (political situation, discussion related to education, and so on) under which the document was produced (Scott, 1990) and the circumstances in which the same document was read and interpreted (Hodder, 2003). For this reason, I considered the combination of documents and newspaper articles essential. I found the press to constitute the most important source of political and social views, providing a day-to-day record of events and valuable information concerning attitudes. Documents and newspaper articles were either compared or used to complement each other by adding information to one another, and provided some insights into the attempts for the development of more inclusive practices in Cyprus, the efforts for a new legislative framework and the process of its official implementation. Of course I had another issue to consider, that of the biased views of newspapers and the fact they often serve the interests of certain political parties and party lines. To offset possible influence of the biased views of newspapers (in periods where there was significant political and educational activity), two or more newspapers, of traditionally opposite political opinions, were used to collect articles.

Although my point of departure for the present research was the idea of discussing the underlying reasons for the government's failure to implement the much promising integration law, the literature offered a theoretical platform that provided a different understanding of policy. The division of the process of policy formulation into the 'making' and 'implementation' of policy derived from a top-down model which implied that only government had the power to 'make policy' (Fulcher, 1999). Both the literature and the preceding documentary research, suggested that policy decisions could be made in any setting outside the structures and control of official government, a setting such as a classroom or a parent-teacher meeting. These arenas constituted a vast range of action or forums for discussion, from central government to places where practice was arbitrated. This framework allowed me to interpret the exclusion of various organizations for disabled citizens or the unions for teachers and parents from the policy discussions for the proposed legal frameworks before 1999, as the attempt of government to minimize external influence, but at the same time as reflecting the ignorance of the government officials of the power of external arenas to influence the process of policy at a later stage. If the government was considered to be the 'top' part of the model of top-down policy implementation, then the schools and classrooms in particular, were the 'down' part.

In the second phase of the project I was concerned with the implementation of the law. Implementation is about the way in which practitioners, who are the people concerned with applying the legal framework, interpret the provision of the law in their everyday actions (Colebatch, 1998). I therefore deemed it necessary to enter schools and observe the ways in which policy was reinterpreted, through daily practices in different arenas within the school. This interpretation of policy was used in illuminating ways. An understanding that policy is made at all levels led me to the observation of policy as a process in schools and the recording of what was happening in everyday life, who was involved in decision-making and the significance of these actions in the process of policy implementation. The use of participant observation allowed me to develop an insider's view of what was happening and form a more informed appraisal of possible actors who influenced daily practice. Lareau and Shultz (1996) argue that participant observation is the method that provides the opportunity to understand day-to-day life in a specific context from the view of the participants, according to their everyday experiences and problems. This technique allowed me to familiarize myself with the participants as well as everyday life in schools, and minimize the possibility of me imposing my own reality on the setting I sought to understand. I concentrated on getting to know respondents and see 'reality' through the participants lenses (Lareau & Shultz, 1996). I studied the behavior, relationships, language and activities of the participants, and with the help of the interviews, I attempted to interpret these, always according to the purposes attached to them and the motives of the actors (Mason, 2002). I employed interview techniques to verify the data recorded in the setting, which included discussing with the interviewees possible arguments or ideas which emerged from observation (Torrance, 2000). Semi-structured interviews were considered appropriate in terms of gaining a broader view of the issues examined and allowed interviewer and interviewee to dwell deep and discuss possible actors influencing policy implementation in the school arena or their own personal role as policy actors. Throughout these conversations I was provided with the opportunity of hearing the concerns of participants, to follow up on their ideas and to clarify their thinking regarding incidents observed. Taken together, both methods (participant observation and semi-structured interviews) provided a richer, more complete and more complex view of social life than either one could offer on its own (Gerson & Horowitz, 2002).

During the process of data collection I was prepared to look for policy actors who through their struggles established their own beliefs and contributed to making policy. I believed that Fulcher's (1999) explanation about the way policy was made in the school was a straight forward process and my concern was to apply this model in the context of Cyprus. Following the first month of collecting data from the three pre-primary schools, I came across what I realized as being contradicting data. In different schools the principal or the class teacher had a substantially differentiated role, which made it impossible for me to decide whether the principal of a school was a policy actor in a position to determine the policymaking procedure or not. This is how the need to enrich this theoretical framework arose. The domination in policy discussions was not preordained due to the position in hierarchy or years of experience. It was important for me to identify in each school, who prevailed in decision-making, who had the power to affect discussion outcomes, who influenced others and legitimized their way of thinking as pertaining to everyday practice, and therefore school policy. I noted that this was rarely the same person, meaning that if in one school the principal was a powerful actor, this role was not to be generalized as being the case in every school. Consequently, in a different school the power holder members might be the teachers or even the parents. The 'winning of struggle' presupposed existence of power in discourse. In adding this notion to the theoretical framework I realized that policy actors had different ways in exercising their power in either maintaining or changing the status quo. The policymaking process involved informed actors who used strategic pursuit to attain their objectives or to deprive their opponents the power of achieving their ends. The need to investigate these strategies and the political interplay between policy actors necessitated the employment of an additional notion, that of micro-politics. This allowed the exploration of the components that informed the political actions of actors and the strategies employed, such as personal ideology, strong feelings about an issue or vested interests. In the framework of this research, the study of micro-politics provided valuable accounts of the subtle, behind the scenes bargaining between the powerful policy actors, who were made up of principals, professionals, teachers and parents, over vested interests and ideological commitments. Micro-politics was understood as being about conflict but also about co-operation and support between school members to achieve their ends. It was about what people think, believe in or have strong feelings about, and generally for what was so often unspoken and not easily observed in a school setting (Blase, 1991). Micro-politics dealt with the realities that school members negotiate on a daily basis.

To sum up, the decisions that shaped my theoretical and methodological framework relied on a broad conceptualization of policy and policymaking. A guiding assumption underpinning this framework was that policy decisions within schools cannot be explained without understanding the underlying political power in the organization. Schools constitute arenas of struggle and thus, it is of great importance to explore how they operate and in what ways policy decisions are made. The final form of this methodological and theoretical framework indicated the need to employ the research methods of participant observation and interviews to understand the daily political interplay, the relationships or potential conflicts between school members, the ideological similarities and diversities among administrators, teachers and parents within schools. This micro-political study of schools aimed to elaborate on the political realities of everyday school life and informed the research project on the basis of how these might guide teachers and other school members in their day-to-day policy decisions in the school arena.

What follows constitutes a personal experience in the identification of the features and outcomes of power being exercised and disability being pathologized. Discussion emphasizes the independence of power in terms of the hierarchical position and the constant alteration of the power holding actors in the process of policymaking, through the employment of a variety of strategies.

WITNESSING THE MEDICAL MODEL AS THE DRIVING FORCE FOR POLICYMAKING

The process of unearthing the strategies used to exercise power and sustain the practices promoted by the medical model was not straightforward. This was due to the fact that they were well embedded in everyday practice. In the study, power brought into examination relations between individuals and allowed the discussion of the structures and mechanisms in which it was exercised. The exercise of power was not simply identifying the relationship between policy actors but was interpreted as a way in which certain actions modified others, or prevented them from happening in order to maintain the status quo.

Having read about the existence and use of techniques of policy actors to achieve their ends (Achinstein, 2002; Ball, 1994; Benjamin, 2002; Kelchtermans, 2007) my approach was not enough to enable a straight forward identification of the ways in which school members were exercising power. Weeks later, having decided on my theoretical framework, I found it difficult to identify the ways in which actors were able to achieve their ends and make policy. Knowledge arising from the documentary analysis (first phase of research) concerning the traditional ways in which professionals, such as educational psychologists, special education teachers or medical personnel, were exercising power and determining the educational future of a child constituted a beginning in this quest. The powerful process of identification of 'needs' and labeling, which the 1999 legal framework introduced along with a number of other practices based on the ideology of individual pathology, allowed the privileged group of professionals to defend and promote their vested interests. Armstrong (2003) argued that professional power was embedded in professional knowledge and practices which were considered to be necessary for the education of children categorized as having 'special educational needs'. After decades of reinforcement of the perspective of intrinsic needs, professional decisions and beliefs were valued as 'regimes of truth' (Foucault, 1980, p. 133) and the power of the professionals to determine school policy was partly a given.

My confrontation with the power of the medical model in policy enactment came through a much unexpected source. At one point during my fieldwork, I was approached by family members and I was asked to explain a letter they had received from their daughter's school. Melani (pseudonym) was born with severe hearing loss and she was in her first year in the elementary school (2006–07). The letter was simply informing the parents that a team of professionals would assess the difficulties of their child on a certain day and that the parents could observe the process if they wished. They were terrified with the idea of this process, but foremost with their inability, as they repeatedly explained, to understand the process or the possible outcomes. I was asked to accompany them, since they felt that they needed someone on their side or, as I understood it, someone who could explain the process. I went along without actually believing in the usefulness of my presence. This is to argue that I strongly believed that the professionals participating in this assessment would actually have no hesitation in explaining the process to the parents. On the contrary, I witnessed the constant effort of the professionals to exclude the parents, emphasizing the professional nature and the necessity of the assessment for the identification of 'needs' and their decision about the most appropriate form of education. The entire experience of assessing the child's 'needs' and the following power struggles between parents, teachers and professionals about the child's education proved illuminating.

One of the first techniques used by professionals, as I was able to identify, was the constant use of professional language amongst them or when they were speaking to the parents: an approach which deprived the parents of the opportunity to understand what was being said and effectively excluded them from the process of decision-making regarding the education of their child. During a multi-professional meeting, in which the parents participated, professionals attempted to persuade them to transfer Melani to another school where she would be able to attend a special education unit, which the professionals argued would facilitate her future reintegration to the mainstream school when she was ready. Both the term of a 'special education unit' and that of 'integration' were unknown words to the parents, as was the new form of education that the parents were asked to choose. I identified the insistence of professionals, along with the lack of information, as techniques that allowed professionals to legitimize their opinion and determine decision-making. The parents were unaware of their right to express objection and although after realizing what this new kind of education included, they were waiting for the next multi-professional meeting in a couple of months' time to express their concerns. This delay legitimized the belonging of the child in the special unit and disempowered the parents in their attempt to change the decision made. From my interpretation this intended delay included a well hidden message about who was in charge of policymaking and the decisions made in the school.

Neither of the techniques identified through these experiences came as a shock to me. The element of surprise was the way in which they were hidden in everyday practices and were easily ignored. What was really unexpected from my side and resulted in a substantial restructuring of my personal understandings and beliefs, was that parents were able to alter to a great extent the outcome of policy decision-making within the school. Parents were able to force professionals to account for their actions by referring to the Special Educational Needs Co-ordinator or the Special Education Inspector of the school, concerning various issues when they believed that their child's rights were at stake. Through formal or informal co-operation with other parents they had the power to transform the decision-making process into a dialogue and make their voice heard. Persistence characterized their every attempt to have a say in the determination of policy. During interviews teachers and principals admitted that sometimes parents had the power to make things happen, even when it was not an area of expertise for the parents. In the case of Melani the absence of a sound proof classroom prevented the speech therapist to conduct her lesson. Whilst the school had waited for the approval of a budget since the previous school year to restructure a certain classroom, the mediation of parents with the Ministry of Education and the Minister himself resulted in the resolution of the issue within two weeks. As perceived by professionals there were topics open for discussion (where the contribution of parents was welcomed) and topics for which the decision-making was based solely on professional expertise. However, it also appeared that parents were being constantly informed regarding their rights and were willing to become more deeply involved in the policymaking procedure. Parents had a 'voice' to promote their rights and their children's rights in opposition to professional expertise, and they expressed their determination to understand the bureaucratic system and effectively contribute. Parents refused to undertake solely the role of helpers in social fairs and were gradually becoming powerful policy actors in the context of the Cypriot education.

Under certain circumstances both principals and teachers proved powerful in the policy discussion. Although hierarchically, the position of principal might have been considered as having an advantage, policymaking was related to the power of the principal to convince teachers to adopt a certain opinion, since the enforcement of their decision on teachers would not be different from the government's attempt to make policy in a top-down model. The first indication I had that the principal of a school was actually a powerless political actor was in the case of Melani. When she was transferred to the special education unit her parents insisted on her constant integration in the mainstream classroom. Despite the principal's agreement and the discussion of the issue between the principal, the parents and teachers (mainstream and special), Melani's integration was occurring not more than three or four hours per week. In the case of this school, the teachers, as more powerful policy actors, simply ignored the principal's instructions in an attempt to protect their own vested interests which included the avoidance of additional planning, use of personal time for co-operation and alternations of teaching methods and material. The principal had never before demonstrated any interest in their work, planning, or difficulties in the classroom, and was, therefore, not only unable to criticize their work, but also unable to offer solutions to practical problems or suggest ways to secure integration. Even at official parent-teacher meetings the principal was simply an attendant, communicating the message that teachers were in charge of what was happening in the school. Frequently Melani's parents were negotiating with her teachers the time schedule of her integration and even when this practice was planned to take place during the principal's teaching in the mainstream classroom the principal was the last to be informed. Notably, what the principal called grant of professional freedom, the teachers characterized as inability to determine school policy.

These experiences were a milestone in the development of my personal thinking and my attempt to conceptualize both the process of policymaking and the deeply embedded ideas of the medical model in the practice of today. My personal involvement and the unique opportunity to follow Melani's case in and out of the school arena, allowed the exploration of power struggles between parents, professionals, principals and teachers and the deconstruction of preconceived ideas about who participates and how policy is made. This experience substantially informed my thinking and exploration of power holder members in the school. Therefore, in the field I was not only pursuing the scheduled weekly teachers' meeting to identify who prevailed in decision-making, but with the permission of the participants I extended my observation to include unscheduled informal discussions between school members, such as the discussions between teachers in the playground or the exchange of ideas between parents and teachers at the school gate during their morning arrival at the school.

FINAL THOUGHTS

Throughout the research journey I understood the importance of the project as being the identification of the existence of both formal (Ministry of Education and Culture) and informal arenas (the assessment and review processes or parents meetings with educational authorities) which had the power to wield in the policymaking process. It was precisely this dismissal of power of arenas and actors outside the formal government which prevented attempts for change in the educational apparatus. Any attempts at change need to extend beyond the governmental legislative terrain. The understanding of the ways in which policy arenas can legitimate the decisions made and determine policymaking and everyday practice need to open 'new possibilities to address the impediments that loom over the attempts for the realization of an inclusive discourse' (Liasidou, 2008, p. 238). The policymaking perspective provided through this personal journey raised, in my opinion, awareness regarding my (and all those working in the inflexible Cypriot education system) powerful role as an educator and a policy actor and the obligation for constant criticism and interrogation of the policies and practices that purport to be inclusive.

I found it astonishing that within the process of continuous struggle for policy formulation involving numerous arenas and actors, none of the discussions or participants aimed to promote change through the restructuring of the school. There was a general lack of recognition over the real need for organizational change of the school and inclusion was perceived as concerned solely with the participation of more students in the mainstream school. Inclusion was not considered to be a synonym of reforming and restructuring the school as a whole or aiming to ensure access for students to the whole range of educational and social opportunities, but as a scheme of integration. The coexistence of the two terms and their interchangeable use as synonyms in the official documents of the MOEC or even the constant confusion over the provisions of the two opposed ideologies in the legal framework of 1999, blurred the boundaries between them. This involves a recognition that in certain circumstances schools support and legitimize difference through a range of pedagogies and a curriculum which bifurcates the education system (Slee, 1997). An important question arises concerning the inadequacy of research in the context of Cyprus: In which way is it possible to attempt to uncover the everyday practices through which the educational system both disables and maintains the current ideologies, stereotypes and fears? The challenge is to detect those habits, beliefs and understandings that remain in place because they are reinforced and eventually become invisible because they are taken for granted (Kinsella & Senior, 2008).

An additional concern was the direct and positive association between formal status and participation in decision-making, which was officially promoted by the procedures of the 1999 legal framework. This factor needs to not only be weakened, but the restructuring of the legal framework needs to encourage new participants. The empowerment of all policy actors could be achieved through the acknowledgement of rights and the respect of everyone's contribution to the process. The empowerment of all could only result in a productive exchange of ideas, co-operative problem solving and the promotion of more inclusive everyday practices. This is of vital importance in bringing about change, and entails the sharing of power which can result in the educational values and practices being influenced by differentiated perspectives, thus becoming more inclusive. In the discussion towards the formulation of a transformative legislation, a number of other issues need to be considered, issues which due to time restrictions and the focus of the research, the study was unable to address. A comprehensive educational legal framework will concern all stages of education: pre-primary, primary and secondary. Even though the current piece of work referred only to issues that arose in pre-primary education, the policymaking process in a differentiated educational stage might encounter various challenges concerning new actors: specifically the role of students as policy actors and the ways in which they can be empowered to participate in the discussion for the determination of their educational future. Potentially, this is likely to significantly alter the balance of power within the policymaking arena and the role of each of the remaining actors.

It is time to focus on how best to implement inclusive education and promote the radical changes it requires (Corbett, 2001). Categorization, discrimination and labeling 'needs' to be recognized as a form of denial of human rights (Kinsella & Senior, 2008). The current law fails to adequately identify that inclusion is concerned with school restructuring and reform of curriculum and practices in relation to all students, and not just concerned with students identified as having 'special educational needs'. Precisely this shortcoming has led to the reproduction of the old education system through the provisions of the 1999 law. There is a necessity to address the issues of the development of the school as a whole, to review the structures and practices of mainstream education and to promote change in the attitudes and the cultures of the mainstream school as a recognition of their possible contribution to the disablement of citizens. An education system based on the principles of the social model would demand the redirection of discourses from the presumption of the 'needs' of a particular student and the reconfiguration of their right to be viewed as equal human beings entitled to mainstream education (Liasidou, 2005). What is essential to remember in this attempt is that change cannot be the outcome of official mandates but the result of people's changing ideas about possible responses to diversity.

REFERENCES

Achinstein, B. (2002). Conflict amid community: The micropolitics of teacher collaboration. *Teachers College Record, 104*(3), 421–455.

Armstrong, F. (2003). *Spaced out: Policy, difference and the challenge of inclusive education*. The Netherlands: Kluwer Academic Publishers.

Ball, S. J. (1994). *Education reform: A critical and post-structural approach*. Buckingham: Open University Press.

Barton, L. (1986). The politics of special educational needs. *Disability, handicap and society, 1*(3), 273–290.

Benjamin, S. (2002). *The micropolitics of inclusive education: An ethnography*. Buckingham: Open University Press.

Blase, J. (1991). The micropolitical perspective. In J. Blase (Ed.), *The politics of life in schools: Power, conflict and cooperation* (pp. 1–18). London: Sage.

Bogdan, R. C., & Biklen, S. K. (1992). *Qualitative research for education: An introduction to theory and methods*. London: Allyn Bacon.

Colebatch, H. K. (1998). *Policy*. Buckingham: Open University Press.

Corbett, J. (2001). *Supporting inclusive education: A connective pedagogy*. London: RoutledgeFalmer.

Drake, R. F. (1999). *Understanding disability policies*. London: Macmillan Press.

Foucault, M. (1980). *Power/knowledge: Selected interviews and other writings 1972–1977*. New York: Pantheon Books.

Foucault, M., & Rabinow, P. (1994). Space, knowledge, and power. In P. Rabinow (Ed.), *The Foucault reader: An introduction to Foucault's thought* (pp. 239–256). London: Penguin Books.

Fulcher, G. (1999). *Disabling policies? A comparative approach to education policy and disability* (2nd ed.). Sheffield: Philip Armstrong Publications (originally published by the Falmer Press in 1989).

Gerson, K., & Horowitz, R. (2002). Observation and interviewing: Options and choices in qualitative research. In T. May (Ed.), *Qualitative research in action* (pp. 199–224). London: Sage.

Hodder, I. (2003). The interpretation of documents and material culture (2nd ed.). In N. K. Denzin & Y. S. Lincoln (Eds.), *Handbook of qualitative research* (pp. 703–716). London: Sage.

Kelchtermans, G. (2007). Macropolitics caught up in micropolitics: The case of the policy on quality control in Flanders (Belgium). *Journal of Education Policy, 22*(4), 471–491.

Kinsella, W., & Senior, J. (2008). Developing inclusive schools: A systematic approach. *International Journal of Inclusive Education, 12*(5–6), 651–665.

87

Lareau, A., & Shultz, J. (1996). Introduction. In A. Lareau & J. Shultz (Eds.), *Journeys through ethnography* (pp. 1–10). United Kingdom: Westview Press.

Liasidou, A. (2005). Cross-cultural perspectives on human rights and inclusive education policies: The case of Cyprus. *Mediterranean Journal of Educational Studies, 10*(2), 97–114.

Liasidou, A. (2008). Politics of inclusive education policy-making: The case of Cyprus. *International Journal of Inclusive Education, 12*(3), 229–241.

Mason, J. (2002). *Qualitative researching*. London: Sage.

McCulloch, G. (2004). *Documentary research in education, history and the social sciences*. London: RoutledgeFalmer.

Oliver, M. (1990). *The politics of disablement*. Basingstoke: Macmillan.

Oliver, M., & Barnes, C. (2012). *The new politics of disablement* (2nd ed.). Basingstoke: Palgrave Macmillan.

Ozga, J. (2000). *Policy research in educational settings*. Buckingham: Open University Press.

Republic of Cyprus (1999). *The 1999 education act for the education of children with special needs (N.113(I)99)*. Nicosia: Government Gazette (in Greek).

Scott, J. (1990). *A matter of record: Documentary sources in social research*. Cambridge: Polity Press.

Slee, R. (1997). Imported or important theory? Sociological interrogations of disablement and special education. *British Journal of Sociology of Education, 18*(3), 407–419.

Symeonidou, S. (2009). Trapped in our past: The price we have to pay for our cultural disability inheritance. *International Journal of Inclusive Education, 13*(6), 565–579.

Torrance, D. (2000). Qualitative studies into bullying within special schools. *British Journal of Special Education, 27*(1), 16–21.

SIMONA D'ALESSIO

7. RESEARCHING DISABILITY IN INCLUSIVE EDUCATION: APPLYING THE SOCIAL MODEL OF DISABILITY TO POLICY ANALYSIS IN ITALY

INTRODUCTION

In this chapter I consider how the adoption of new theoretical perspectives in researching education can impact upon the development of inclusive education research and the dissemination and impact of research findings. To exemplify this, I draw upon my doctoral study conducted in Italy between 2004 and 2008 and I discuss the changes which occurred in the research process as a result of embracing a new ideology. Specifically, the chapter describes the research process, which applied the social model of disability to the investigation of educational policy. Most of the reflections presented here derived from a research project conducted in a small Italian town situated in the northern part of the country. The purpose of the research was aimed at critically analyzing the extent to which the Italian educational policy known as *integrazione scolastica* (school integration) could be considered an inclusive policy (D'Alessio, 2008).

Discussion illustrates the tensions and contradictions I experienced as a young non-disabled female researcher undergoing a shift in thinking while conducting inclusive education research. In particular, the chapter identifies how the engagement with critical readings derived from the social model of disability and a radical position (see Cigman, 2007) of inclusive education influenced the thinking behind the research and determined a change in the research trajectory and purpose. I focus on how a new theoretical framework influenced my research decisions: framing of the research questions; sampling; conceptualization of the notions of disability, schooling and inclusion; and the choice of the methods used to conduct the study and analyze the data.

In the first part of the chapter I focus on the area of research chosen to conduct my study and I provide a brief outline of existing research methodologies used to research disability in education. The second section is concerned with a short description of the Italian context, in which my research was conducted, and the topics I investigated and why. In the third section I illustrate how my research underwent a slight detour from its original plan as a result of the application of new theoretical frameworks and how such ideologies influenced my research decisions and design. In the fourth section I provide examples of how my beliefs and values

S. Symeonidou and K. Beauchamp-Pryor (Eds.), Purpose, Process and Future Direction of Disability Research, 89–106.

were scrutinized and how such scrutiny changed my views. In this section, which is divided into four subsections, I also present relevant findings which emerged from my study and I explain how these impacted upon the development of inclusive education in Italy. Finally, I discuss the importance of the writing-up process and I comment on how the process reflects the experiences of the researcher.

RESEARCHING DISABILITY IN EDUCATION

The importance of the social model of disability has been crucial for changing the perspective of those conducting disability research in general and in education in particular. This has been particularly relevant since the development of emancipatory research (Barnes, 1992; 2003; Mercer, 2002; Oliver, 1992; Zarb, 1992): a research paradigm that modified the way in which research in Disability Studies has been carried out. The paradigm, supported by paradigm, supported by the social model of disability, emphasized a transformation of the power relations between the researcher and the researched (Barnes, 2003), with the aim of removing any form of discrimination against disabled people by disseminating research findings that could benefit research participants (hence disabled people).

Although more than two decades have passed since the introduction of emancipatory research, this research perspective is still in a precarious state (Barnes, 2003). Nevertheless, it has produced significant changes in the research process. Such changes are particularly evident in issues concerning the choice, design, strategies and purposes of doing disability research as well as the incorporation of disabled people's views. A good example of these changes can be found in the attempts to incorporate the views of disabled people in international reports and initiatives, such as the perspectives of Disabled People's International in the last version of the *International classification of functioning, disability and health* produced by the World Health Organization (WHO, 2001). Similarly, the European Agency for Development in Special Needs Education has promoted three initiatives, the first held at the European Parliament in Brussels in 2003, the second held in Lisbon within the European Union Presidency of Portugal in 2007 and the third held at the European Parliament in Brussels in 2011 (see European Agency for Development in Special Needs Education, 2005; 2007), to provide pupils identified as having special educational needs with a space to voice their concerns in relation to education and employment in front of European and national policymakers. Whilst these initiatives may still present limitations, such as questions concerning the actual power that disabled people have to place items onto the policymakers' agenda, or to promote alternative constructions of disability and thus initiate impacts upon institutions, they nevertheless indicate that a new awareness about the role and the rights of self-advocacy and self-determination of disabled people is slowly developing (see also the *Convention on the rights of persons with disabilities*, United Nations, 2006).

Disability research (Clough & Barton, 1995; 1998) and, in particular emancipatory research, has successfully addressed issues about research accountability, validity and effectiveness. By doing so, disability research now occupies a place within other forms of so-defined 'mainstream' research strategies, and promotes the emergence of new research forms, such as narrative research (Armstrong, 2003) and action research (Armstrong & Moore, 2004), which have recently challenged conservative research forms and produced new reflections and developments (Goodley, 2005; Goodley & Moore, 2000).

Although my study cannot be defined as emancipatory, the research possesses an emancipatory quality. Being a woman, although not specifically a feminist researcher (Oakley, 1981), I acknowledge the influence of gender as a category of analysis and organization of my research. As argued by Cohen, Manion and Morrison (2007), feminist research is more routinely being associated with a research approach that: deconstructs traditional commitments to truth, objectivity and neutrality; uses a multiplicity of research methods; involves the people being researched; positions the researcher him/herself as relevant data; and addresses the issue of power relations in the research production.

It is not surprising therefore that being a female researcher influenced, and possibly determined, my reflective turn and my desire to develop reciprocity with participants hearing, listening and equalizing the research relationship – doing 'with' instead of 'on' research subjects (Pillow, 2003, p. 179) and most importantly, bringing into the research process an emancipatory element: that is, research should be empowering for all participants including the researcher (Usher, 1996). In addition, a feminist perspective presents some similarities with the emancipatory research conducted by disabled people and their allies, as the experience of women, like that of disabled people, is for the first time researched from another point of view. A perspective that breaks with the traditional masculine picture of reality and the positivist research approach that usually empowers white, male dominated research communities at the expenses of other social groups that remain silenced (Cohen, Manion & Morrison, 2007).

In general, it can be argued that my research falls within the themes addressed in Disability Studies and more specifically in the field of Disability Studies in Education (DSE) (Connor et al., 2008). This is because it is rooted in the principle that disability research is about instigating change, either on the life conditions of disabled people, and/or to stimulate policymakers, researchers, practitioners and disabled people alike to take responsibility when carrying out disability research. As a non-disabled researcher working within the DSE paradigm, the adoption of a new framework of thinking changed the way in which I positioned myself in relation to different research informants. It also determined a focus on the investigation of the existing power relations in place in education and in policymaking settings. Although my research did not manage to unhinge existing power relations, it nevertheless brought to the fore a deeper understanding about the life conditions of disabled pupils disabled pupils in schools and a new awareness on the need to theorize and investigate disability as a social construct. To do so, my research drew upon an application of the social model of disability (Oliver, 1990; 1996; 2009; Oliver & Barnes, 2012). It is important to acknowledge that the social model of disability is not a theory and that it should not be treated as such without stumbling into critiques (see Shakespeare & Watson, 2002; Terzi, 2005; 2008). However, the social model became crucial to challenging the perspective from which researchers interpret and explain phenomena. This will become evident in the next section in which I describe how the adoption of a new ideological perspective influenced the way I conducted research including the introduction of new modalities of investigation within the Italian research arena.

UNDERSTANDING THE ITALIAN CONTEXT AND IDENTIFYING THE RESEARCH TOPIC

Since the 1970s, the Italian education system became particularly renowned among researchers studying the area of special needs education, because Italy had enacted an innovative and unique policy that had allowed disabled pupils to attend their local schools along with their non-disabled peers. At a European level, while other countries and international bodies were still investigating whether it was possible to integrate disabled students into mainstream classrooms, for example with the Helios projects in the 1980s (Struiksma & Meijer, 1989), Italy was already exploring ways of how to improve the quality of education for disabled people in integrated settings (D'Alessio, 2009). For this reason, many scholars (Booth, 1982; Buzzi, 1993; de Anna, 1997; Ferri, 2008; Hegarty, 1987; Meijer, 2010; Meijer & Abbring, 1994; Mittler, 2000; O'Hanlon, 1995; Organization for Economic Co-operation and Development, 1994; 2005; Segal & Gautier, 2003; Thomas & Loxley, 2001) indentified that the Italian policy of *integrazione scolastica* was a progressive approach within the field of inclusive education and a policy that required international recognition.

Despite the implementation of this policy, some students, in particular disabled students, were still facing forms of discrimination and marginalization in Italian schools and in the employment sectors, as a result of societal barriers and prejudices. I was working as a support teacher in secondary schools at the end of the 1990s and I was often faced with a feeling of uneasiness due to the perpetuation of discriminating practices (despite the best intentions of classroom and support teachers to do otherwise). Similarly, local tribunals reported that parents were appealing against schools and local education authorities concerning the lack of extra facilities allocated to mainstream schools and the perpetuation of segregating attitudes. Recently, national newspapers reported that special schools, which were almost dismantled since 1977, were slowly being reconstituted (although in different shapes and forms), partly driven by parents' complaints about the inadequacy of mainstream schools (Bomprezzi, 2010) and partly because special schools had never really been closed down (Barbieri, 2007), especially for learners with sensory impairments (see European Agency for Development in Special Needs Education, 2008).

Although the policy of *integrazione scolastica* is considered a fundamental standpoint for the dismantling of segregated education, and consequently, for the development of inclusive education in Italy (Canevaro, 2002; 2007; Canevaro &

Mandato, 2004; Ianes, 2005), many contradictions arose which urged researchers to investigate further the reasons why some forms of exclusion are perpetuated (D'Alessio, 2008; 2009; 2011a; 2012).

In the next section I reflect on the process of investigating forms of exclusion and discrimination and how it impacted upon the process of researching itself.

A DETOUR FROM THE ORIGINAL RESEARCH PLAN

As a social researcher interested in the development of an inclusive school system, I decided to conduct an ethnographic study of two lower secondary schools. My research was not commissioned by disabled people's organizations, policymakers or academic departments, but originated in personal preoccupations for the future of education, especially for those pupils who were at risk of exclusion as a result of the way in which school and society were structured and organized.

At the start of my study, my intention was to provide evidence that identified the policy of *integrazione scolastica* as an inclusive policy. I strongly believed that other countries could rely on the experience and practice developed within the Italian context in order to develop the process of including disabled students into mainstream schools and, in the longer term, to improve the overall quality of their education systems. At the same time, I was not aware that my research approach was based on outdated assumptions about the meaning of disability which were enshrined within dominant discourses about schooling and education.

During my initial visits and observations at two secondary schools (chosen as my case studies), I was driven by a belief that disability was a personal deficit that needed to be compensated for by medical intervention and the work of specialized professionals. Similarly, I failed to question the meaning and purpose of schooling and education. Also my interpretation of inclusive education was mostly concerned with the process of mainstreaming disabled pupils into mainstream schools, with little or no awareness that the notions of integration and inclusion were not synonymous.

In the last decade, as a result of the use of the *International classification of impairment, disability and handicap* (ICIDH) (WHO, 1980) and subsequently of the *International classification of functioning, disability and health* (ICF) (WHO, 2001), and compared to other Western countries, Italy had already developed a more complex interpretation of the notion of disability. The language used to refer to disabled people was 'people in a situation of disability', rather than disabled people. From an Italian position, disability was considered as a condition of social disadvantage in which people with impairments were living and represented those who were dependent upon the provision of environmental support (D'Alessio, 2007). However, it is important to note that in the Italian context the term 'handicap' was originally used instead of 'disability' and such a term is still encountered in national legislation. Basically, the starting point remained the person and their 'malfunctioning' and the need to adjust according to an ableist interpretation of normality (D'Alessio, 2006). Hence, I was not sensitive of political issues about disability and/or the importance of understanding who was making the decisions, for whose benefit and why: basically, I was not concerned with issues of power.

Given the above considerations, my original research question was concerned with providing examples of how inclusive education could be implemented into schools by drawing on the features of two Italian schools applying the policy of *integrazione scolastica*. However, although my main interest was about inclusive features, during my fieldwork I started to record forms of micro-exclusion (Nind et al., 2005), which were taking place in the schools implementing mainstreaming policy. Consequently, the focus of my study underwent a detour: rather than proving how *integrazione scolastica* could represent a way of implementing inclusive education in Italy, I started to investigate why despite the passing of this progressive policy, disabled pupils and pupils who differentiated from the perceived norm were still experiencing difficulties at school, and why support teachers were considered as 'the only guardians' of disabled children. I became aware of exclusion mechanisms and of the existence of discriminating discourses embedded within major policy documents and legislative measures, which were related to the process of integration, but were not perceived as such. The latter and other forms of micro-exclusions replaced the original focus of my research. Such replacement resulted from a change in the theoretical framework as the following section will indicate.

HOW A NEW THEORETICAL UNDERPINNING INFLUENCED MY RESEARCH DECISIONS

In this section I describe the impact of the adoption of a new ideological perspective on the research undertaken. The effects of such an impact did not result in a single event but in a series of epiphanies (D'Alessio, 2008) that modified the way in which I theorized disability, understood inclusive education, interpreted policy and policy analysis and enabled me to identify existing disabling discourses and mechanisms of micro-exclusions.

As argued by Parker and Baldwin (1992, p. 197), the way in which the research has been 'informed' may influence how it is carried out (for example the research questions, the choice of methods and design, the form of analysis and the pattern of dissemination of its findings) and, I would add, it may also determine the level of its impact. While visiting the schools, I began reading the works of social modellists (in particular Michael Oliver, Len Barton, Colin Barnes and Paul Abberley) and inclusive education scholars (such as Len Barton, Felicity Armstrong, Roger Slee, Julie Allan, Mel Ainscow and Jenny Corbett). I also engaged with the works of Gramsci (1971) and Foucault (1977), in order to address issues around discourses, power, control, hegemony and human agency, which became fundamental in understanding the issues around power relations in the policymaking process and the construction of the notion of disability.

The works of Gramsci and Foucault were fundamental for the research undertaken as their thinking provided support to the change of perspective foreseen by the social model of disability: Gramsci (1971) suggested ways of considering the sociological implications of education for the wider society; Foucault (1977) suggested ways of questioning the reasons why societies needed to adopt particular regulatory systems (for example naming, categorization, classification and labeling) as means of understanding and of controlling particular social groups. Drawing on these thinkers, it was possible to understand the intrinsic nature of mainstream schools beyond the enlightened vision of teaching and learning and to interrogate the conditions under which education systems operated and power was exercised. Therefore, the change of trajectory was fundamentally the result of looking at things through the lens of a new ideology influenced by the social model of disability and inclusive education principles.

From an individual/medical model perspective, the focus of research is on the examination of individual deficiencies, and the modifications required to support the 'integration' of a disabled child in mainstream settings. From a social model perspective, sociological analyses needs to focus on the institutions that house and segregate disabled people and contribute to the creation of a social stigma and on the reasons behind these actions (Stone, 1984). By drawing on the social model of disability, my observations did not focus on the individual experiences of disabled pupils, the provision allocated to favor their development, the work of specialized teachers or the interaction between specialized teachers and the pupil with a 'statement of special educational needs'. My observations were concerned with the organization and structures of mainstream schools, general teachers and the consequences of adopting traditional forms of curriculum, pedagogy and assessment, despite the increasing diversity of the student population. Finally, a sociological approach led me to seek explanations that did not only concern the special support for disabled children and the allocation of extra resources to schools, but to understand why some children were required to adopt a 'special' identity (such as 'special educational needs pupils') in order to be provided with additional resources necessary to exert their rights to education (D'Alessio, 2008).

Although different theoretical frameworks (such as the medical/individual model versus social model) may arguably be equally valid, they nevertheless focus on different aspects, providing different explanations and related solutions for similar phenomena (for example 'disability' and 'school failure'). This statement is exemplified in Table 7.1 in which I speculate how different theoretical approaches may produce different understandings of the same phenomenon (such as its focus) and stimulate different actions (such as its explanations and solutions).

With this in mind, when delving into the social model of disability and the works of the scholars previously identified, questions were raised about the nature of schooling and disability and the distortions with which they were constructed. It was at that time that a series of epiphanies took place and became fundamental to my undertaking:

– A new theorization of disability.
– A new understanding of the concept of inclusive education.

- A new understanding of the process of policy analysis.
- A growing awareness that discrimination and exclusion were still taking place in the schools implementing *integrazione scolastica* despite more than thirty years passing since the progressive policy had been enacted.

Table 7.1. An example of a paradigm shift from a medical/individual model of disability approach to a social model of disability approach and its consequences.

	Object of study		
Models of disability	*Focus*	*Explanation*	*Solution*
	Phenomenon under investigation: disability		
Medical model of disability.	Person and individual deficit.	Personal problem ('personal tragedy'): biological dysfunction.	Rehabilitation and economic support (e.g. incapacity benefits and pensions).
Social model of disability.	Act of discrimination and social oppression.	Perpetuation of forms of exclusion and injustice based on the way in which society is structured.	Removal of societal barriers (e.g. promoting universal design), challenge of discriminatory policies and cultural biases.
	Phenomenon under investigation: student failing at the exam		
Medical model of disability.	Student failure.	Student is not intelligent enough or he/she does not study.	Failing, disruption and/ or repetition of the school year.
Social model of disability.	No learning is taking place.	Teaching and learning practice is not effective for all students	Revising/transforming existing teaching and learning approaches.

In what follows, I turn to explain my new understandings around the aforementioned issues.

The Theorization of Disability

Drawing on the social model of disability I started to study and understand disability as a complex phenomenon. The social model, as named within the field of Disability Studies (Barnes, Oliver & Barton, 2002; Barton & Oliver, 1997), is characterized by three key elements that can be briefly summarized as follows: first, the difference between impairment (biological condition) and disability (social condition); second, a distancing from the medical model of disability, which locates limits within the person's 'deficits'; third, the condition of oppression experienced by disabled people in society. Within this approach disability is understood as a social construction: consequently, it is necessary to go beyond the impairment to look at the disabling conditions of society that affect the lives of disabled people (D'Alessio, 2008, p. 57).

Given the above considerations, I questioned the definitions of disability derived from the individual/medical model of disability, which did not differentiate between impairment and disability. As a result of this approach, I interrogated the usages of international classification manuals, such as the ICIDH (WHO, 1980) and the ICF (WHO, 2001), and how these definitions contributed to the construction of the notion of disability within medical discourses. The medical model (which is still embedded in these classification manuals), mostly viewed the 'solution' to the 'problem' in terms of medical intervention (for example, rehabilitation and normalization procedures), and when medical intervention was not possible the focus turned to economic compensation rather than promoting societal change (Barnes, Mercer & Shakespeare, 1999).

I am very much indebted to the works of Michael Oliver: his historical analysis of the concept of disability and his materialistic critique of the normalization principle (Oliver, 1990; 1996; 2009; Oliver & Barnes, 2012). Oliver made a case that the individual/medical model of disability was associated with the idea of disability as a 'personal tragedy', which suggested that disability was some terrible chance event, which occurred at random to unfortunate individuals. Thus, disability was theorized as a form of 'dysfunctioning' or something 'which did not work' inside the person. As a consequence of this perspective, disabled people often blamed themselves and felt responsible for their personal and social condition. Consequently, the view implied that disabled people contributed to the construction of their own condition as passive citizens (pure recipients of humanitarian, caring and welfare policies). Clearly, such a vision was strongly reinforced in Italy by the Catholic religion and its discourses about acceptance towards God's will, which resulted in economic dependence and mere acceptance of ones life conditions.

Although the works of Oliver were very critical towards the medical domain, he did not deny the importance of medical interventions and the work of medical professionals, the latter being fundamental to improving the life of disabled people. Similarly, whilst I supported the social modellists approach, I did not want to underestimate the importance of specialized support and medical intervention. Such a position was particularly relevant, I argued, when researching disability in low-income or so-defined developing countries (for example some African states) where different strategies were required to fight the lack of medical care, access to health and rehabilitation services. The problem with the medical/individual model, especially in Western countries, was that it limited the attempts to question whether there were other reasons, which might have determined, or alternatively which could have improved, disabled people's life conditions beyond a medical intervention (the latter being often useless for chronic diseases). Much in agreement with Oliver, I questioned whether it was the role of medical professionals to decide policies for disabled people (for example housing, education and employment) and whether such professions needed to instead deal with health issues only.

The Concept of Inclusive Education

The work of inclusive education scholars allowed me to understand that inclusive education had nothing to do with the inclusion of pupils with special educational needs, but with transforming mainstream schools into inclusive communities for all pupils. Nevertheless, the focus on the experience of schooling of disabled pupils remained central for two main reasons:

> [firstly, because] disabled pupils continued to experience discrimination at school, and their experience of political and social struggle could be relevant in understanding how exclusion manifests itself in society today (Armstrong and Barton, 2001). Secondly, because exclusionary practices became more visible 'along the lines of class, 'race', ethnicity and language, disability, gender and sexuality and geographic location' as such. (Abberley, 1992, p. 143)

This statement was crucial as it illustrated how the limits of the education system became more tangible when studied in relation to the education of marginalised sections of the population. My research made a case that inclusive education was not about meeting the needs of a 'vulnerable' minority in a mainstream setting, but was concerned with answering fundamental questions about: what type of school was needed to meet the requirements of all students; and, most importantly, what the goals of education ought to be. The focus was, therefore, on the type of schooling required for the twenty first century and on the complexity of the interpretation of concept of inclusion itself (D'Alessio, Donnelly & Watkins, 2010; D'Alessio & Watkins, 2009).

A new understanding of inclusive education contributed to the replacement of the subject of my research with another (Fulcher, 1995). Rather than researching disabled pupils and the way of responding to their 'deficits', I started to detect mechanisms of exclusion, which were often disguised as forms of inclusion, but which impeded some students from participating actively in the process of learning. Therefore, mechanisms of categorization and individualization, which pathologized disability and constructed it as a form of personal tragedy (Oliver, 1990; Oliver & Barnes, 2012) slowly became the object of my observations. For instance, I questioned the process of certifying disabled students in order to provide them with all the necessary adaptations, accommodations and resources in mainstream schools (see for example the Italian legislation known as the *Legge Quadro*, N.104 [Italian Republic, 1992]) and the writing of the 'Individual Educational Plan' as an inclusive procedure. Likewise, I began to interrogate the custom of using national statistics identifying the number of disabled pupils integrated into mainstream classrooms as evidence of 'inclusiveness'. I questioned the use of statistics as an indicator of the good quality of the application of the policy of *integrazione scolastica*. In my thesis I argued that statistical figures (which indicated that almost all disabled pupils were educated in mainstream classrooms in Italy), needed to be investigated as a way of assembling and organizing reality by experts and, therefore, they were a topic of research themselves, rather than a source for evaluating integration or inclusion:

We should thus not look for an answer to the question 'what is the true number of disabled people?' Rather we should recognize, as Oliver has pointed out in relation to disability (Oliver, 1983) and other writers have argued in more general and wide-ranging ways (Hindess, 1973; Irving et al., 1979) that all statistics are constructed by particular people in particular social and historical contexts for particular purposes, and can only be understood as such. (Abberley, 1992, p. 143)

With this in mind, I argued that inclusive research was not about focusing on the number of pupils identified as having special educational needs placed in mainstream classrooms, but about identifying statistical evidence of how many discriminating policies and barriers to participation were still in place in our education systems (such as the existence of segregating policies, categorizing procedures, and the absence of inclusive teacher training). Unfortunately, current statistical analyses did not seem to address the complexity of the process of categorizing and assessing disabled pupils and did not appear to engage with the consequences of labeling disabled students as 'others', supposedly with the best intentions of doing them good (such as for the provision of extra resources and personnel).

The Process of Policy Analysis

The engagement with policy analysts (for example Ball, 1993; Fulcher, 1989) led me to address the investigation of the policy of *integrazione scolastica* from a sociological perspective. Rather than exploring technical and functional issues to find out about the application of arguably 'well-designed' policies at a school level, I decided to investigate the ideology within which a policy initiative was enshrined and to question the underpinning taken for granted discourses and practices. Therefore, the policy of *integrazione scolastica* was not only studied as an unproblematic humanitarian policy, which allowed a previously marginalized section of the population to participate actively in society, rather its political, economic and social origins were taken into account and investigated (D'Alessio, 2011a).

Research decisions included the investigation of issues about the process of how a policy was formulated (for example, the language used and the discourses articulated in the policy text); which ideological framework influenced policymaking (for example, the medical or social model of disability); the wider social context in which the policy was made (for example, the role of actors and the historical time and place); and the relations of power from which the policy resulted (for example, who made the decisions and with what purposes). It was with these considerations in mind that I identified the reasons why the policy of *integrazione scolastica* was still embedded in the same theoretical premises of special needs education and the individual/medical model of disability paradigms.

Thanks to my new understanding of policy and the policymaking process, I argued the case that *integrazione scolastica* was not an inclusive policy, thus reversing the original assumption with which I began my investigation. It was not appropriate for educational policies to be evaluated solely from an operational level, and their application at a school level, but policy analysts needed to engage with issues of power relations, especially those operating within the process of policymaking. The paradigm shift fostered the possibilities of critiquing the ideological foundations of mainstream education and brought to the fore that a reductionist notion of *integrazione scolastica* (stemming from a special needs education mindset), had prevailed over a systemic notion of *integrazione scolastica*, which aimed to challenge the education system (D'Alessio, 2009; 2011b).

Disabling Discourses and Mechanisms of Micro-exclusions

Although the most striking factors of exclusion had almost been completely dismantled in Italy (such as segregated institutions) exclusion was (and is) still resilient. Exclusion is not a straightforward notion and it may take different shapes, such as the perpetuation of practices that have been taken for granted and have remained unnoticed for many years, together with the reproduction of disabling discourses which are embedded in dominant policies.

In the schools chosen as case studies, I was often faced with micro-policies, for example teachers' behaviors, practices and language, which provided evidence of forms of micro-exclusions, often camouflaged as inclusive features. In particular, I witnessed episodes of withdrawing which involved disabled students being taught in special units by their support teachers or teaching assistants; the maintenance of special units within mainstream schools; the reproduction of the practice of delegation (disabled students shifted into the hands of support teachers only); the writing of individual educational plans as a form of diagnostic assessment; the perpetuation of disabling discourses which constructed disabled pupils as 'others' and therefore provided with a parallel form of schooling within the same 'space' (D'Alessio, 2012). Specifically, by drawing on the works of Foucault, I identified a series of discourses that were meant to promote inclusive education, which instead reproduced forms of exclusion. These discourses included: the discourse of 'need'; the discourse of school change; and the discourse of celebrating diversity (D'Alessio, 2008). As far as the discourse of celebrating diversity was concerned, all teachers interviewed in my study reported about the need to value diversity and students' potentialities. However, whenever I entered the classrooms it was difficult to find examples of how diversity was being valued by class teachers in terms of teaching and learning routines (such as pedagogy, curriculum and assessment). Similarly, the discourse of need was always associated with pupils experiencing difficulties at school. In this way not only were students transformed into needy individuals lacking something, but also school systems and routines remained untouched. Finally, the discourse of school change was used only in relation to the education of disabled pupils, rather than triggering a fundamental change in the way in which mainstream schools were organized.

RESEARCHING THE FIELD AND RESEARCHING THE SELF

Much in agreement with the accounts of Len Barton about the research process (in Allan & Slee, 2008) my research was an unsettling and disturbing process characterized by many pitfalls. As shown in the previous sections, I struggled with my previous positions and assumptions in conducting research in general and inclusive education research in particular. However, by being self-critical, I learnt that the research process can be a rewarding journey teaching a great deal not only about the topic, but also about yourself and the reasons which influenced why you decide to conduct a specific type of study.

As the four epiphanies described in the previous section (the theorization of disability; the concept of inclusive education; the process of policy analysis; the investigation of disabling discourses and mechanisms of micro-exclusions) indicate, my ideological position shifted from a special needs education paradigm into an inclusive education paradigm. Slowly, but not without difficulties, I constructed my identity as a social researcher in inclusive education, both via the research decisions taken and the writing-up process. This development took place because my research method was characterized by a process of self-enquiry, and a re-examination of taken for granted assumptions and self-evident ideas that I used to perceive as natural. The use of reflexivity, along with auto-ethnography and evocative personal writings, has increasingly been recognized within the social sciences and mainstream academic publications as a way of writing qualitative research (Davies, 1999; Denzin, 1997; Ellis & Bochner, 2000; Marcus, 1994; Pillow, 2003). This new approach is particularly relevant for inclusive education research, where reflexivity becomes a modality of conducting research (Slee & Allan, 2001), as inclusion 'starts with ourselves' (Allan, 2005, p. 282). It was only by undergoing such a reflective process that I was able to disentangle myself from a dominant deficit model of disability and explore new forms of investigating policies and practices related to *integrazione scolastica*.

The adoption of the principles of Inclusive Education and Disability Studies in Education also impacted upon the style used to write up my research. Writing becomes a journey that reflects the researcher's political and moral position. This was evident in the style and language used to write my research: for example, I prioritized the account in the first person and avoided the use of the language of special education (see D'Alessio, 2008). I made this decision not only to help the reader to familiarize with the process undergone by the researcher and to bring to the fore personal positions, beliefs, biases and limits that could not have been expressed otherwise, but also to break with a positivist research tradition that considered the researcher primarily as distant in relation to his/her work. On the contrary, as it is also argued by Allan and Slee (2008) researchers are not neutral to the research production and it is necessary to articulate ones' assumptions and presuppositions, in order to add to the validity and reliability of the research conducted.

In conclusion, whilst I positioned my study within Disability Studies in Education, when I consider the impacts of my findings, I realize that my research can also be aligned with the 'school improvement/reform paradigm' (Allan & Slee, 2008, p. 16). I identified this latter paradigm because firstly, my research did not focus only on issues around disability, although the notion of disability remained crucial to understand the process of inclusive schooling; secondly, my interviews with disabled people and students occupied a peripheral position and so did their voices; and thirdly, there was no radical change in the process of research production, as I remained the one orchestrating the study. Nevertheless, I managed to provide research participants with a high level of freedom to draw on their accounts rather than offering them my understandings of integration. For instance, when I interviewed teachers I proceeded with open-ended questions and I sought to position myself as a learner.

With hindsight, my research process strengthened the findings of my work as any alternative research design, I believe, would have proved to be inappropriate. This reflection derives from the fact that it was only by conducting my research in the way I did that I managed to challenge my presuppositions and outdated assumptions about school integration and education in general. On the other hand, if I were to conduct my research again, I would provide more space for the inclusion of disabled people's voices as informants of my study.

Research in *integrazione scolastica* needs to promote development in the area of inclusive education research by supporting a paradigmatic shift (Kuhn, 1970) from special education to inclusive education. Such a shift is crucial, otherwise discursive formations will perpetuate existing power relations and will reproduce a mono-dimensional construction of *integrazione scolastica* emanated from a historically situated frame of reference, that of special needs education of the nineteenth century (Foucault, 1970; 1972; 1978; 2003; Scull, 1979; Stiker, 1999).

CONCLUSION

This chapter has shown how critical engagement with new theoretical principles and values derived from inclusive education, social model of disability and Disability Studies in Education have clearly impacted upon research decisions. Much in agreement with Clough and Barton (1995), research needs to use knowledge to challenge the forms of oppression disabled people experience, rather than reproducing a system of domination, especially in the educational domain. Although it is not possible to clearly identify specific examples of how my study impacted upon the experiences of disabled pupils at schools or on the process of policymaking as promoted by emancipatory research, I hope that my research will influence the work of other researchers by stimulating debate and dialogue between interested parties (Barton, 1992). Similarly, in the Italian setting, I hope that my research is made available and discussed by the widest possible audience (Parker & Baldwin, 1992) in order to trigger the transformation of both research procedures and school routines, and that the change I have experienced as a researcher others will experience.

There is a clear need in the Italian context to research education, and disability within education, by bringing into the process of research disabled people and their allies in order to break with a tradition of research that speaks on behalf of disabled people. In addition, more research needs to be conducted in the area of inclusive education going beyond the issue of 'mainstreaming' disabled people in classrooms to challenge dominating discourses about disability, education and schooling, which currently influence policymaking and school practice. In Italy, only a small group of independent researchers (such as Angelo Marra, Roberto Medeghini, Giuseppe Vadalà, Enrico Valtellina and myself), both disabled and non-disabled (Medeghini et al., 2013), are currently attempting to break with traditional ways of researching disability and bring about issues of change[1].

Undertaking disability research in the area of inclusive education can be a very powerful action, it may produce similar shifts in thinking, forge new types of research and as my research attempted, it can wake up 'the conscience from the lethargy of rhetoric' (D'Alessio, 2008, p. 261).

NOTE

[1] For information about the development of Disability Studies in Italy and the foundation of the *Italian Journal of Disability Studies*, please go to http://gridsitaly.net/

REFERENCES

Abberley, P. (1992). The significance of the OPCS disability surveys. *Disability, Handicap and Society, 7*(2), 139–155.

Allan, J. (2005). Inclusion as an ethical project. In S. Tremain (Ed.), *Foucault and the government of disability* (pp. 281–297). Michigan: University of Michigan Press.

Allan, J., & Slee, R. (2008). *Doing inclusive education research*. Rotterdam: Sense Publishers.

Armstrong, D. (2003). *Experiences of special education. Re-evaluating policy and practice through life stories*. London: Routledge.

Armstrong, F., & Barton, L. (2001). Disability, education and inclusion. In G. L. Albrecht, K. D. Seelman & M. Bury (Eds.), *Handbook of disability studies* (pp. 693–710). Thousand Oaks: Sage.

Armstrong, F., & Moore, M. (2004). *Action research for inclusive education: Changing places, changing practices, changing minds*. London: Routledge Falmer.

Ball, S. J. (1993). What is policy? *Text, Trajectories and Toolboxes in Discourse, 13*(2), 10–17.

Barbieri, P. (2007). Welfare e democrazia: Tra partecipazione ed esclusione. *Paper presented at the Stati Generali della Disabilità. Rome, Italy.*

Barnes, C., (1992). Qualitative research: Valuable or irrelevant? *Disability, Handicap and Society 7*(2), 115–124.

Barnes, C. (2003). What a difference a decade makes: Reflections on doing 'emancipatory' disability research. *Disability and Society, 18*(1), 3–17.

Barnes, C., Mercer, G., & Shakespeare, T. (1999). *Exploring disability. A sociological introduction.* Cambridge: Polity Press.

Barnes, C., Oliver, M., & Barton, L. (Eds.). (2002*). Disability studies today*. Cambridge: Polity Press.

Barton, L. (1992). Introduction. *Disability, Handicap & Society, 7*(2), 99.

Barton, L., & Oliver, M. (Eds.). (1997). *Disability studies: Past, present and future*. Leeds: Disability Press.

Bomprezzi, F. (2010*). Perché ritornano le scuole speciali. Corriere della sera. [Why special schools are coming back].* Retrieved on April 18, 2010, from http://archiviostorico.corriere.it/2010/aprile/18/Perche_ritornano_scuole_speciali_co_9_100418095.shtml

Booth, T. (1982). Integration Italian style. In C. Gravell & J. Pettit (Eds.), *National perspectives. Unit 10.* Milton Keynes: Open University Press.

Buzzi, M. I., (1993). Handicap e Europa: Verso paradigmi comuni di integrazione. [Handicap and Europe: Towards common integration paradigms]. *Valore Scuola, 188*(XVI), 3–7.

Canevaro, A. (2002). Pedagogical, psychological and sociological aspects of the Italian model. A methodological preamble. *Conference paper presented at the Mainstreaming in Education Conference*, Rome, June 13–15.

Canevaro, A. (Ed.). (2007). *L'integrazione scolastica degli alunni con disabilità. [The integration of pupils with disabilities]*. Trento: Erickson.

Canevaro, A., & Mandato, M. (2004). *L'integrazione e la prospettiva 'inclusiva'. [Integration and the inclusive education perspective]*. Rome: Monolite Editrice.

Cigman, R. (2007). *Included or excluded? The challenge of the mainstream for some SEN children*. London: Routledge.

Clough, P., & Barton, L. (Eds.) (1995). *Making difficulties. Research and the construction of SEN*. London: Paul Chapman Publishing.

Clough, P., & Barton, L. (Eds.) (1998). *Articulating with difficulties. Research voices in inclusive education*. London: Paul Chapman Publishing.

Cohen, L., Manion, L., & Morrison, K. (2007). *Research methods in education*. London: Routledge.

Connor, D. J., Gabel, S. L., Gallagher, D. J., & Morton, M. (2008). Disability studies and inclusive education – implications for theory, research and practice. *International Journal of Inclusive Education, 12*(5), 441–45.

D'Alessio, S. (2006). *Disability and certification. A new perspective in Innovazione Educativa*. IRRE ER, 5, 22–28. Retrieved on July 23, 2012, from http://kids.bo.cnr.it/irrsaeer/rivista/nazionale5-606.pdf

D'Alessio, S. (2007). Made in Italy: Integrazione scolastica and the new vision of inclusive education. In L. Barton & F. Armstrong (Eds.), *Policy, experience and change: Cross cultural reflections on inclusive education* (pp. 53–73). London: Springer.

D'Alessio, S. (2008). *A critical analysis of the policy of integrazione scolastica from an inclusive education perspective. An ethnographic study of disability, discourse and policy making in two lower secondary schools in Italy*. PhD thesis. Institute of Education. University of London.

D'Alessio, S. (2009). *Integrazione scolastica*, 30 years on. Some critical reflections and suggestions for the development of inclusive education in Italy. *La nouvelle revue de l'adaptation et de la scolarisation, IN SHEA Revue, Hors Série 5*, 51–65.

D'Alessio, S. (2011a). *Inclusive education in Italy. A critical analysis of the policy of integrazione scolastica*. Rotterdam: Sense Publishers.

D'Alessio, S. (2011b). Decostruire l'integrazione scolastica e costruire l'inclusione in Italia. [Deconstructing integration and constructing inclusion in Italy]. In R. Medeghini & W. Fornasa (Eds.) *L'educazione inclusive. Culture e pratiche nei contesti educative e scolastici: Una prospettiva psicopedagogica [Inclusive education. Cultures and practices in inclusive school settings]* (pp. 69–94). Milano: FrancoAngeli.

D'Alessio, S. (2012). *Integrazione scolastica* and the development of inclusion in Italy: Does space matter? *International Journal of Inclusive Education*, DOI:10.1080/13603116.2012.655495

D'Alessio, S., & Watkins, A. (2009). International comparisons of inclusive policy and practice: Are we talking about the same thing? *Research in Comparative and International Education Journal, 4*(3), 233–249.

D'Alessio, S., Donnelly, V., & Watkins A. (2010). Inclusive education across Europe: The move in thinking from integration to inclusion. *Revista de Psicologia y Educacion 1*(5), 109–126.

Davies, C. A. (1999). *Reflexive ethnography*. London: Routledge.

de Anna, L. (1997). Pedagogical, curricular and classroom organisation in Italy. In OECD (Ed.), *Implementing inclusive education* (pp. 91–95). Paris: OECD.

Denzin, N. K. (1997). *Interpretive ethnography. Ethnographic practices for the 21st century*. Thousand Oaks: Sage.

Ellis, C., & Bochner, A. P. (2000). Autoethnography, personal narrative, reflexivity. Researcher as Subject. In K. N. Denzin & S. Y. Lincoln (Eds.), *Handbook of qualitative research* (pp. 733–769). Thousand Oaks: Sage.

European Agency for Development in Special Needs Education. (2005). (V. Soriano, M. Kyriazopoulou, H. Weber & A. Grünberger (Eds.), *Young views on special needs education*. Odense: European Agency for Development in Special Needs Education. Retrieved April 20, 2012, from http://www.european-agency.org/publications/ereports/young-views-on-special-needs-education/young-views-on-special-needs-education.

European Agency for Development in Special Needs Education. (2007). (V. Soriano, Ed.) *Young voices: Meeting diversity in education*. Odense: European Agency for Development in Special Needs Education. Retrieved April 20, 2012 from: http://www.european-agency.org/publications/ereports/young-voices-meeting-diversity-in-education/young-voices-meeting-diversity-in-education.

European Agency for Development in Special Needs Education. (2008). *SEN data*. Retrieved April 20, 2012, from http://www.european-agency.org/country-information/italy/national-overview/sne-data

Ferri, B. A. (2008). Inclusion in Italy: What happens when everyone belongs. In S. L. Gabel & S. Danforth (Eds.), *Disability and the politics of education. An international reader* (pp. 41–52). New York: Peter Lang.

Foucault, M. (1970). *The order of things: An archeology of the human sciences*. London: Tavistock Publications.

Foucault, M. (1972). *The archeology of knowledge*. New York: Pantheon.

Foucault, M. (1977). *Discipline and punish* (A. Lane, Trans.). London: Penguin.

Foucault, M. (1978). *The history of sexuality. An introduction* (R. Hurley, Trans. Vol. 1). London: Penguin.

Foucault, M. (2003). *Abnormal lectures at the collège de France, 1974–1975* (G. Burchell, Trans.). London: Verso.

Fulcher, G., (1995). Excommunicating the severely disabled: Struggles, policy and researching. In P. Clough & L. Barton (Eds.) *Making difficulties. Research and the construction of SEN* (pp. 6–24). London: Paul Chapman Publishing.

Fulcher, G., (1989). *Disabling policies? A comparative approach to education policy and disability*. London: Falmer Press.

Goodley, D., (2005). Empowerment, self-advocacy and resilience. *Journal of Intellectual Disabilities, 9*(4), 333–343.

Goodley D., & Moore, M. (2000). Doing disability research: Activist lives and the academy. *Disability and Society 15*(6), 861–882.

Gramsci, A. (1971). *Selections from the Prison Notebooks* (Q. Hoare & N. G. Smith, Trans.). London: Lawrence & Wishart.

Hegarty, S. (1987). *Meeting special needs in ordinary schools*. London: Cassell.

Ianes, D. (2005). *Bisogni educativi speciali e inclusione. Valutare le reali necessità e attivare le risorse. [Special educational needs and inclusion. How to assess real needs and activate resources]*. Trento: Erickson.

Italian Republic. (1992). *Legge-Quadro per l'Assistenza, l'Integrazione sociale e i diritti delle persone handicappate. [Framework law for the assistance, integration and rights of handicapped people]*. Gazzetta Ufficiale, February 17, 1992 n. 39. Retried on July 23, 2012 from http://www.edscuola.it/archivio/norme/leggi/l104_92.html

Kuhn, T. S. (1970). *The structure of scientific revolutions*. Chicago: University of Chicago Press.

Marcus, G. E. (1994). What comes (just) after 'post'? The case of ethnography. In K. N. Denzin & S. Y. Lincoln (Eds.), *Handbook of qualitative research* (pp. 563–574). Thousand Oaks: Sage.

Medeghini, R., D'Alessio, S., Marra, A., D., Vadalà, G., & Valtellina, E., (Eds) (2013). Disability studies. Emancipazione, inclusione scolastica e sociale, cittadinanza. Trento: Erickson

Meijer, C. J. W. (2010). *Special needs education in Europe: Inclusive policies and practices. Zeitschrift für inklusion, 2*. Retrieved on May 9, 2010, from http://www.inklusion-online.net/index.php/inklusion/article/view/56/60

Meijer, C. J. W., & Abbring, I. (1994). Italy. In C. J. W. Meijer, J. S. Pijil & S. Hegarty (Eds.), *New perspectives in special education. A six-country study of integration* (pp. 9–23). London: Routledge.

Mercer, G. (2002). Emancipatory disability research. In C. Barnes, M. Oliver & L. Barton (Eds.), *Disability studies today*. (pp. 228–249). Cambridge: Polity Press.

Mittler, P. (2000). *Working towards inclusive education*. London: David Fulton.

Nind, M., Benjamin, S., Sheehy, K., Collins, J., & Hall, K. (2005). Methodological challenges in researching inclusive school cultures. In K. Sheehy, M. Nind, J. Rix & K. Simmons (Eds.), *Ethics and research in inclusive education. Values into practice* (pp. 30–61). London: RoutledgeFalmer.

O'Hanlon, C. (Ed.). (1995). *Inclusive education in Europe*. London: David Fulton Publishers.

Organization for Economic Co-operation and Development (OECD). (1994). *The integration of disabled children into mainstream education: Ambitions, theories and practices*. Paris: OECD.

Organization for Economic Co-operation and Development (OECD). (2005). *Students with disabilities, learning difficulties and disadvantages. Statistics and indicators*. Paris: OECD.

Oakley, A. (1981). Interviewing women: A contradiction in terms. In H. Roberts (Ed.), *Doing feminist research* (pp. 241–263). London: Routledge and Kegan Paul.

Oliver, M. (1990). *The politics of disablement*. Basingstoke: Macmillan.

Oliver, M. (1992). Changing the social relations of research production. *Disability, Handicap & Society, 7*(2), 101–114.

Oliver, M. (1996). Understanding disability: From theory to practice. London: Macmillan.

Oliver, M. (2009). *Understanding disability: From theory to practice* (2nd ed.). London: Palgrave.

Oliver, M., & Barnes, C. (2012). *The new politics of disablement* (2nd ed.). Basingstoke: Palgrave Macmillan.

Parker, G., & Baldwin, S. (1992). Confessions of a jobbing researcher. *Disability, Handicap & Society, 7*(2), 197–203.

Pillow, W. S. (2003). Confession, catharsis, or cure? Rethinking the uses of reflexivity as methodological power in qualitative research. *International Journal of Qualitative Studies in Education, 16*(2), 175–196.

Scull, A. T. (1979). *Museums of madness. The social organisation of insanity in 19th century England*. London: Penguin Books.

Segal, P., & Gautier, M. (2003). *La compensation du handicap en Italie*. Paris: CTNERHI.

Shakespeare, T., & Watson, N. (2002). The social model of disability: An outdated ideology? *Research in Social Science and Disability, 2*, 9–28.

Slee, R., & Allan, J. (2001). Excluding the included: A reconsideration of inclusive education. *International Studies in Sociology of Education, 11*(2), 173–192.

Stiker, H. J. (1999). *A history of disability* (W. Sayers, Trans.). Michigan: University of Michigan Press.

Stone, D. A. (1984). *The disabled state*. London: Macmillan.

Struiksma, C., & Meijer, F. (Eds.). (1989). Integration at work. *Conference paper presented at the first European community conference on handicap and education, Pedologisch Instituut Rotterdam*, October 25–27.

Terzi, L. (2005). Beyond the dilemma of difference: The capability approach to disability and special educational needs. *Journal of Philosophy of Education, 39*(3), 443–458.

Terzi, L. (2008). *Justice and equality in education*. London. New York: Continuum.

Thomas, G., & Loxley, A. (2001). *Deconstructing special education and constructing inclusion*. Buckingham: Open University Press.

United Nations. (2006). *Convention on the rights of persons with disabilities*. Retrieved on May 5, 2008, from: http://www.un.org/esa/socdev/enable/documents/tccconve.pdf

Usher, R. (1996). Feminist approaches to research. In D. Scott & R. Usher (Eds.), *Understanding educational research* (pp. 120–142). London: Routledge.

World Health Organization (WHO). (1980). *International classification of impairment, disability and handicap*. Geneva: WHO.

World Health Organization (WHO). (2001). *International classification of functioning, disability and health*. Geneva: WHO.

Zarb, G. (1992). On the road to Damascus: First steps towards changing the relations of disability research production. *Disability, Handicap & Society, 7*(2), 125–138.

KAREN BEAUCHAMP-PRYOR

8. RESEARCH REFLECTIONS: SECURING INCLUSION FOR DISABLED STUDENTS IN WELSH HIGHER EDUCATION

INTRODUCTION

This chapter reflects on my experience of completing doctoral research: a study which set out to develop a framework towards securing inclusion for disabled students in higher education (Beauchamp-Pryor, 2008; 2013). I discuss the research process and identify factors that influenced the direction of my project and the approaches I adopted. The first part of my chapter initially considers the reasoning behind my choice of research topic. In particular, I address the impact of my personal experience of disability on the research area and my motivation to undertake the study. A brief overview of the project and methodology is provided before reflecting on the underpinning principles which guided my study. These principles focused on: the purpose of social research and my role as a researcher; the process of adopting an emancipatory research paradigm; issues of 'insider' and 'outsider' status; difficulties of researching-up; and the process of dissemination. My conclusion provides a final reflection on my project and considers the future direction of my work.

RESEARCH TOPIC

My choice of research topic was directly influenced by my personal experience of impairment and disability: a division which treats impairment from a medical model position as personal limitation, and disability from a social model position as socially produced inequality and dependency (Barnes & Mercer, 2003; Oliver, 2009; Oliver & Barnes, 2012). In the following short account I reflect on the influence of growing up as a visually impaired child, my early educational experiences, and my subsequent return to education in my mid thirties.

I was born with congenital cataracts, which until recently were inoperable. My grandfather, mother and sister were all visually impaired and in the early years of my childhood I thought visual impairment was 'normal'. For the first few years of my education (in the mid 1960s) I went to Norfolk House, a private school in Cardiff: I enjoyed school, made friends and I am unable to remember an occasion where I was treated differently from any other child at school. However, my experiences in education were about to drastically change when the school closed and I was subsequently enrolled at the local junior school. School life became difficult and

S. Symeonidou and K. Beauchamp-Pryor (Eds.), Purpose, Process and
Future Direction of Disability Research, 107–120.

I began to realize what it meant to be different to other children. I believe these differences were reinforced by the actions of teachers in the classroom. In particular, I remember the way teachers drew attention to my inability to participate in lessons. My sister was attending Chorleywood College, a grammar school for blind and visually impaired girls, and was in her final year of studying for 'A' levels. It was decided that I too should apply to Chorleywood College and my parents organized additional tuition in preparation for the entrance exam. At the age of ten I was accepted, but with my acceptance came unhappiness of being away from home. After eighteen months my parents made the decision that it would be better for me to be at home and to attend the local comprehensive school. Initially I was placed into a remedial class and I suddenly went from receiving a high standard of education to none at all. I was later moved into a mainstream class and for the rest of my secondary education I was anxious not to draw attention to myself and to make sure that I 'fitted in'. I did not excel and my ability was hidden by dominant perceptions about disability as inability.

During the early 1990s, I decided to return to further education: I was interested in equine studies and managed to complete National Vocational Qualification level one and two (a work based qualification reflecting the skills needed to carry out a job effectively), but realized very quickly when I enrolled for level three, that I would be unable to manage with the classroom and laboratory based work. I discussed my difficulties with special educational needs support staff, but rather than trying to help resolve the problems I encountered, the suggestion was made that I enroll on an Access (a course designed to prepare students who wish to study at a higher educational level). In the previous year, a visually impaired student had completed the Access course and the lecturers had some experience of 'coping' with a visually impaired student and, therefore, it was felt they would be able to 'cope' with me. The change in direction was to prove a new beginning and the start of my academic career. I thrived and wanted to learn more about each of the subject areas covered on the course, and I was keen to go to university. I was amazed at the level of provision that was on offer in higher education: books could be photocopied and enlarged or recorded on to tape, computer software enabled scanning and reading of material, note-takers for lectures were available and even transport to and from university could be arranged.

In 1998 I commenced my undergraduate studies at Swansea University and even though I felt anxious, as any other student, I was keen to make the most of every opportunity. Initially, however, the promised support did not materialize and although I sought help from the lecturers in the form of copies of overheads and back copies of notes, support proved to be variable. The difference in response towards disability by individual lecturers and across departments became evident and, even at this early stage, I began to recognize factors that impeded my inclusion. I made the decision to change degree scheme from Psychology to Social Policy, and at the same time proceeded with an official complaint. Prior to 2001 there was no legal protection against the discrimination of disabled students in higher education, but my complaint highlighted the differing responses between academic departments.

It was during this time, that I was introduced to the social model of disability by Robert Drake. In our early discussions, I found it difficult to comprehend the concept of the social model: from experience I knew that simple changes could enable inclusion and participation, but I also believed that ultimately my lack of vision was personal and individualized. Two books written by visually impaired academics were later to act as a catalyst in furthering my understanding about the experience of disability: the first was Colin Barnes' book *Disabled people in Britain and discrimination* (1991) and the second Sally French's edited volume *On equal terms* (1994). I was able to relate to their personal experiences and understood the issues they discussed. I began reading more widely and was influenced by Michael Oliver's (1990) arguments about the political and policy response towards disabled people, together with his combined work with Jane Campbell (1996). Their arguments, supported by Drake's (1996) study, identified the lack of voice experienced by disabled people in the development of legislation and policy: arguments which influenced the direction of my research.

RESEARCH PROJECT AND METHODOLOGY

As a direct result of my personal experiences within higher education, I was intrigued to know how other disabled students faired: how included did they feel and what were the factors that influenced these feelings? I selected a case study university in Wales, which I chose mainly because of the high level of provision offered to disabled students, together with the large number of disabled students studying at the university. Initially questionnaires were sent out to 491 disabled students registered with Student Support Services, and 116 were completed and returned. The student questionnaire was designed to gather data about: past and present educational experience; choice of university and course; the provision of additional assistance within academic departments; examination support offered; effectiveness of disability support services; participation in student activities; knowledge of legislation; and involvement in the direction of policy and provision. The questionnaire identified those students willing to participate further in the research and 23 students were chosen to reflect a cross section of impairment categories and a range of backgrounds and characteristics such as gender, ethnicity, age, experience of different courses and subject areas, and levels of study. Interviews were largely unstructured, which was an important decision, as the flexibility allowed issues to be discussed that were important to the students, and as a result the data covered many aspects of university life. The unstructured approach will be returned to later in the chapter when considering 'an emancipatory paradigm'. Research participants were assured of anonymity and pseudonyms were provided.

Interviewing was carried out between 2001 and 2003 and in addition to the students, extensive interviewing was undertaken with managerial, administrative and support staff working in a wide range of departments across the university, which included planning, estates, admission and marketing, equal opportunities, widening participation, staff development, disability support services, examination support, the international office, and accommodation. In addition six disability co-ordinators were interviewed within academic departments. My questioning reflected my interest in identifying the impact of legislation and policy on the experiences of disabled students and, therefore, I sought to determine: the general understanding of disability legislation; and dominant views about disability.

Within the Welsh context I examined reports, reviews and policy documents and compared the Welsh response with policy and provision in England and Scotland. I undertook a survey of Welsh higher educational institutions and sent questionnaires to each of the 13 institutions in Wales: eight were completed and returned by disability support staff. I wished to identify the steps being taken by institutions to comply with legislation and to determine dominant perceptions about disability.

Within the UK context I undertook an analysis of legislative and policy processes to understand more fully the competing tensions that existed between policymakers, higher education providers, traditional charities and disabled people. The analysis involved scrutiny of archival material linked to UK legislative and policy development and the interviewing of key informants. Key informants included: a leading disability academic; a disability activist who was a member of the Disability Rights Task Force (the DRTF was set up by the Labour Government in 1997 to take forward their manifesto commitment to secure comprehensive and enforceable civil rights for disabled people); and two disabled student representatives participating in policy consultation.

UNDERPINNING PRINCIPLES

A number of important principles guided the direction of my study and these included: a commitment to challenge oppression; adopting an emancipatory approach; researching from an 'inside' position; researching-up and identifying the views of those who influenced the direction of policy and provision; and ensuring dissemination of findings.

Challenging Oppression

My first underpinning principle reflected my research concern about the purpose of social research and my role as a researcher. This was because conventional ethnography was criticized for neglecting the causes of oppression and for being aloof from political practices. Theorists, such as Habermas, claimed that because social oppression was inherent in modern capitalist societies, valid social research was only attainable through a committed struggle against oppression (Davies, 1999, p. 61). Within disability studies, it was argued, research had played a role in the oppression of disabled people (Abberley, 1992; Barnes, 1996; Hunt, 1981; Oliver, 1992; Rioux & Bach, 1994) and as Oliver (1992) asserted, little research challenged the social oppression and isolation experienced by disabled people or initiated policies to significantly improve the quality of their lives. It is now almost fifty years since Becker (1967) argued that researchers needed to declare whose side they were on in the research process, and today, research independence is progressively viewed as a mythical entity:

> Researchers should be espousing commitment not value freedom, engagement not objectivity, and solidarity not independence. There is no independent haven or middle ground when researching oppression: academics and researchers can only be with the oppressors or with the oppressed. (Barnes, 1996, p. 110)

For some social scientists this line of reasoning was too simplistic in approach: as Hammersley (1995) claimed, the world cannot be divided neatly into those who are oppressors and those who are oppressed, as many people would be classified as both. For example, there are cross-cutting sources of oppression for disabled people, such as gender (Morris, 1996) and race (Vernon, 1997). As a disabled person, these debates were important to me, but it was evident that disability research had in the past compounded, rather than improved the inequality experienced by disabled people within society.

In addition, I questioned whether it was possible for me to be a detached observer in the research process: I had experienced oppression and discrimination and brought these experiences to the research. It was these experiences as an 'insider', which enabled me to identify factors that influenced equality and inclusion. As Wheatley reasoned:

> Ethnographic relations, practices and representations as well as the metaphors we use to make sense of them are contextually contingent – their character is shaped by who we look at, from where we look, and why we are looking in the first place. (1994, p. 422)

Arguably, no research can be completely free of bias, and I constantly monitored my values and experiences at each stage of the project. I was anxious not to jeopardize the validity of my research, because I believed the findings had the potential to challenge dominant perceptions about disabled students. Therefore, whilst my research position was clear (I was on the side of the oppressed), I was concerned that I may be perceived by those involved in developing disability policy and provision, as a disabled student with a skewed or one-sided view of what it was like to be a disabled student in higher education. In practice this meant that throughout the research I tried to distance myself from situations which arose within the university and in policy development: for instance, I was invited to contribute to an inquiry about complaints received from disabled students, which I declined. With hindsight I was probably over cautious, because debatably whatever position I took as a researcher, due to my disabled student status, I was unlikely to have been perceived as objective. Issues of conflict around my research position as a disabled student will be addressed further in my discussion of 'insider research' and 'researching-up' later in the chapter.

An Emancipatory Research Paradigm

My second underpinning principle was about the importance of challenging the inherent inequality between researcher and researched within the research process. Oliver (1997) identified six ways in which an emancipatory research paradigm was able to contribute to combating the oppression of disabled people: firstly, the providing of a factual and undistorted account of the experiences of disabled people; secondly, a redefining of disability away from an individual or medical model; thirdly, challenging ideology and methodology of dominant research paradigms; fourthly, utilizing a methodology commensurate with emancipatory research; fifthly, offering an account of the collective experience of disabled people; and finally, the monitoring and evaluation of services controlled by disabled people.

The principles discussed by Oliver were important to me and I set out to provide an accurate account of the experiences of students who participated in my study. I adopted a social model approach throughout (redefining disability as a consequence of attitudinal, environmental and institutional barriers) and because of my approach I was able to identify policy and practice which led to inequality and exclusion. During the early part of my study, my first supervisor Ken Blakemore, who later retired, suggested that I question the impact of impairment on student experience. At the time I adamantly argued that my research was not about questioning the relationship between individual and social factors. However, more recently I re-examined my position and I have begun to appreciate that focusing entirely on social factors can be exclusionary. For instance, understanding the significance of impairment effects (the experience of living with impairment) and the psycho-emotional impact of disablism (for example, issues around self-esteem and personal confidence), as discussed by Thomas (1999; 2007), also impact on the experience of inclusion. Moreover, I have increasingly recognized that 'rights' is about understanding differing individual experiences, which is important in achieving equality and inclusion (Beauchamp-Pryor, 2012a). The relationship between equality, social factors and individual factors is illustrated below in figure 8.1 (Beauchamp-Pryor, 2012a, p. 183). However, even with hindsight, I would not have changed my research position because disability

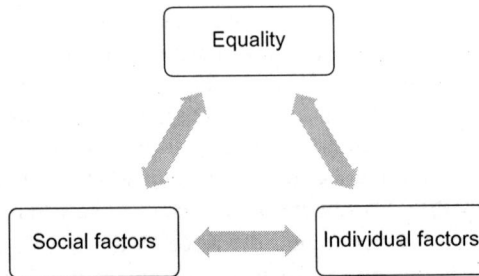

Figure 8.1. Towards an equality framework.

was not understood at that time as an equality issue: arguably discussion of individual factors can only exist within an equality framework.

Oliver's third and fourth criteria were concerned with shifting control of the research process from the researcher to the researched: the knowledge and skills of the researcher are placed at the disposal of the researched, resulting in a shared approach in the design, implementation and analysis of the research. My study was for a PhD and, at that time, I considered that it was impractical to involve students due to my own time constraints and other students' commitments. I did, however, consult on a regular basis with four disabled students whose input I valued. With hindsight, I realize that failing to involve disabled students was about my lack of confidence and lack of skills. In future research plans, my aim would be to ensure that disabled people are more vocal in the research process as I believe this not only empowers disabled people, but strengthens the research project.

In complying with Oliver's remaining criteria, my study provided an account of the collective experiences of disabled people and although I did not include the monitoring and evaluation of services controlled by disabled people, I did consider the representation of disabled people in policy and practice which included the different approaches of organizations controlled by disabled people and those representing disabled people. As identified in earlier studies (Campbell & Oliver, 1996; Drake, 1996), my findings similarly identified that the government continued to rely on those who purported to represent disabled people: consequently, the lack of voice experienced by disabled student representatives was evident (Beauchamp-Pryor, 2012b).

Oliver also detailed three essential principles in an emancipatory methodology: 'reciprocity, gain and empowerment' (1992, p. 111). Again these principles were of central importance and directed the research design, as considered below.

I was influenced by feminist critiques, which asserted that formal survey type interviewing was an appropriate research method in researching women. Oakley (1981) argued for less structured research strategies which challenged traditional hierarchical relationships between interviewer and interviewee. Interview techniques, for Oakley, were about building a rapport, with the interviewer not only asking questions, but welcoming and answering the respondent's questions, as opposed to traditional objectivity. I was concerned about the unequal relationship between myself and the students I interviewed, and I realized that even by adopting less formal approaches the relationship would not be completely equalized. In addition, I was aware that knowing when to share my own experience was also necessary, as similarly considered by Vernon (1997) who drew on Ribbens reasoning:

> ...we should ...take our cue from the person being interviewed for they may not always wish to know and it may detract them from talking about themselves. (1989, p. 584)

Reflecting on the interview process, the sharing of experience was important because many of the participants had felt isolated and unable to share their experiences with anyone else. The isolation experienced was evident when interviewing Paul: when Paul received my research questionnaire he was relieved that an opportunity had arisen for him to be able to talk to another disabled student. Until this time he had not had any contact with any other disabled student on campus:

> I haven't spoken to a disabled student on campus. I don't see anybody. …I honestly wanted to have a chat with some other [disabled] students to see if they are feeling the same, if they have had the same experience as me.

Oakley detailed a further level of reciprocity in the development of long-term friendships and I too found that this happened. In many respects, as Vernon (1997, p. 169) also identified, the forging of 'lasting friendships' is inevitable when there are so many shared experiences.

Reflecting on who gained, the benefits were threefold: personal; participant; and political. At a personal level I benefited because the project was for a PhD. I also gained from the experience of sharing and listening to the experiences of other disabled students. In the same way, I hoped that those students who participated in the research would also gain and, ultimately, be empowered. Karl (1995) asserted that the first step to empowerment was about treating research participants as equals. The experience of many disabled people is not to have been treated as equals and as Vernon claimed, treating research participants as equals boosts their 'self-confidence and self-esteem' (1997, p. 172). I also hoped that the setting-up a disability society or forum would be a further way in which students could empower themselves. The forum initially proved successful: firstly, in providing an opportunity for students to develop friendships; secondly, in identifying and discussing issues that were important to them; and thirdly, in creating dialogue between the students and those involved in the implementation of policy and provision within the university. However, in later years the forum disappointingly folded, partly due to lack of priority within the Student Union towards disability issues, and partly due to the lack of free time available to students to contribute to the organization of the forum. Notably, disabled students lacked spare time and at interview described additional pressures in managing full-time study, for example organizing course work to be taped or transcribed into Braille. These pressures were not unrepresentative of disabled students more generally. For instance, both Magnus (2006) at a Norwegian University and Riddell, Tinklin and Wilson (2005) in England and Scotland identified similar findings.

Whilst participants involved in the project did not directly gain from changes in policy and provision, they recognized that their contribution to the study had the potential to bring about change: 'I hope that things will change now, not for me, but for future students' (Paul). From the outset my research aim was to influence the direction of policy and provision to ensure that future students felt included in higher education. Later in the chapter I discuss the dissemination process and I will return to the benefits of my research in challenging dominant policy approaches.

'Insider' Research

My third underpinning principle concerned the importance of carrying out research from an 'inside' position. Reimer contended that as an 'inside' researcher, familiarity within a research situation can be sociologically beneficial and suggested that the approach:

> ... enables the researcher to use familiar situations or convenient events to this advantage. They know rather than know about their area of study. They are insiders. (1977, p. 469)

I was an 'insider' in two main ways: firstly, I was a disabled student researching the experiences of other disabled students; and secondly, I was actively involved in two organizations representing disabled people. As an 'insider', I may have been criticized for being too close to the research process, but on the other hand I attained an insight into the research that other researchers may have found difficult to achieve. I was aware of studies which had examined the opinions of disabled people on research and identified that participants were often concerned about non-disabled researchers ('outsiders') misrepresenting their experiences (Duckett & Pratt, 2001; Kitchin, 2000). As John, a participant in Duckett and Pratt's study, suggested 'you have to live with it [disability] to fully know what it means' (2001, p. 828). Other findings from the Kitchin (2000) research also identified that disabled people often limited what they told non-disabled researchers, due to possible embarrassment, lack of empathy, or fear over possible reassessment of benefits/services.

These apprehensions were important to me and as I set out to interview students I hoped that those involved in my project would feel that I understood the experiences they discussed. However, in discussions about feminist research approaches, Luff (1999) reasoned that a shared experience does not necessarily mean a shared outlook. I did not always share the same views as other disabled students, but as the findings unfolded the shared experience of being disabled was important. There were differences based on gender, race, and age, and as a consequence, differences in outlook and experience were evident: hence the need to share and explore a wide range of experiences, which identified similarities in understanding of what it meant to be included or excluded.

Since completing my doctorate, I revisited my position as an 'insider' in greater depth. The questioning process was triggered and driven by the uncertainty I experienced following successful eye surgery in terms of my identity and my role as a disabled activist and researcher. I concluded that the experience of a shared struggle against oppression blurred the divide between disabled/'insider' and non-disabled/'outsider':

> To be an 'insider', therefore extends beyond the immediate category of impairment to an experience based on inequality and exclusion. Moreover, 'insider' status is about understanding the experience of inequality and exclusion, whether this is based on disability, race, gender, age, sexual

orientation, gender-reassignment or religion. It is the shared experience of oppression that underpins 'insider' status. Whilst an 'outsider' may not have experienced oppression directly, it is the commitment and struggle to confront oppression and inequality that unites 'insiders' and 'outsiders'. (Beauchamp-Pryor, 2011, pp. 14–15)

Researching-up

My fourth underpinning principle reflected the process of researching-up: a process which shifts the research focus from those who lack power to those with power (Oliver, 1992). It is argued that little research is carried out on those who hold power (Oliver, 1992) and it was critical therefore, not only to examine the experiences of disabled students, but also to consider the perspectives of those who influenced student experience. My research position changed to researching-up, and I was in the position of interviewing those employed in influential positions. At first this experience was quite daunting, as I recognized the sensitivity of a disabled student/ researcher interviewing those directly involved with disability policy and provision.

At an institutional level, I tried to put those interviewed at ease and reassure them over issues of confidentiality. Throughout the process I felt anxious about how I was perceived by staff, whether managerial, administrative or academic. On reflection, I now appreciate I was in a powerful position, but at the time because of my lack of confidence and lack of experience, I thought my position was weak. The response towards my research varied, with no clear divide apparent between the three staff groupings: some members of staff welcomed the study and trusted me implicitly, and others did not. The trust was evident in the enthusiastic long discussions with staff at interview about disability policy and provision, and the distrust clear when interviewees were restrained and detached from interview questions. Moreover, the mistrust was observable when a senior manager at the case study university contacted my supervisor for draft copies of my research findings: a request that was refused. It is difficult to assess whether a non-disabled researcher would have been trusted more by those who mistrusted me, or whether a non-disabled researcher would have been mistrusted by those who trusted me.

I largely concealed my interest in equality and rights and in discussions with managerial, administrative and academic staff I focused more generally on the impact of legislation and policy. I was concerned that I would be perceived within the university as a disability activist and that, as a result, staff would be unwilling to participate in my research: a concern which was arguably justified, because of the dominant perceptions about disability in terms of 'inability'. For instance, at a university meeting a member of staff suggested the importance of understanding disability from a social model perspective and the reaction of committee members immediately worked to alienate his position. Therefore, had I not concealed my social model position I suspect that I might have found it difficult to secure the co-operation of university staff.

Similar dilemmas were evident in my regular contact with those developing policy at a national level. Whilst I remained careful in how I worded correspondence when seeking details about policy development, the process of raising questions and seeking information in itself highlighted the issues of potential inequality and exclusion which I was addressing. However, there were times when I met people who were very supportive of the issues I was raising and in particular, I recall the support from one senior policy advisor at the Disability Rights Commission. Interestingly, through his openness I began to understand and appreciate more fully the process of policy negotiation and co-operation at all levels of policy development: from Whitehall (government administration) to disabled people.

Dissemination

My final underpinning principle was about the dissemination of my findings and recommendations. In order to influence the future direction of policy and provision it was crucial that the findings and recommendations were disseminated at an international, national, institutional and student level. On completing the project I felt daunted about how to successfully achieve the dissemination of my findings. The external examiner at my viva voce examination, Len Barton, recommended that I sought further funding to build upon my research findings and I decided to apply for an Economic and Social Research Council Postdoctoral Fellowship. My application was successful and under the supervision of my mentor, Anne Borsay, I was able to develop and strengthen my skills: in writing for publication; in presenting papers at conferences and seminars; and in preparing a grant application for further research funding. As a direct result the validity of my work has become increasingly recognized within disability studies and inclusive education.

Dissemination has been effectively achieved through the presentation of papers at conferences (Degrees of Independence Conference, 2009; and the Nordic Network of Disability Research Conference, 2009) and seminars (University of Cyprus, 2012; Centre for Disability Studies at Leeds University, 2010; Institute of Education University of London, 2010; Linkoping University, 2010; and Swansea University, 2009). My conference and seminar papers have generated issues for those attending and the feedback has been constructive in helping me to formulate further research questions. These questions will be returned to when I consider my future directions at the end of the chapter. My findings were also presented at the case study university and were received positively by managerial and administrative staff, but the changes in legislation were likely to have influenced the positive response to my paper. Since then I have been able to provide advice to the university about ways to secure the involvement of disabled students in policy development. I did not, however, disseminate my findings to the students who participated in my study, which I now regret. With hindsight, whilst I reasoned that students would leave the university prior to the completion of findings, the failure to present and discuss my work was a missed opportunity not only for the students, but also for me in not seeking their views. An issue which is further discussed in the conclusion 'reflections and future directions'.

REFLECTIONS AND FUTURE DIRECTIONS

I was driven to complete my research by the powerful accounts provided by students and it was their experiences which gave me the impetus to complete each stage, whether fieldwork, analysis or writing-up. The students entrusted me to tell their stories about why they felt excluded within higher education and I had a duty and responsibility to explain and develop awareness and understanding of the inequality experienced by them. Throughout the project I worried about my lack of confidence, inability and inexperience, and I was concerned that I would ultimately fail them. Similarly as a postdoctoral research fellow, I was anxious to disseminate my findings effectively and as I undertook new ventures I continued to be anxious about whether I had the ability to complete each task required of me.

I regret that I did not involve students more fully in the early development of the project and during the research process. I now appreciate that sharing views at an early stage about the research approach would have strengthened my study. Since completing the project and listening to the views of other disabled students about my research, I realize the value and importance of differing perspectives. Moreover, my failure to disseminate ongoing findings with the students participating in my study is regretful. In preparing a recent grant application for further research funding I argued that the involvement of students was central to the development of the study and in future projects I will ensure that I secure student involvement.

Reflecting on my approach and questions addressed within the study two important questions continue to remain outstanding. Whilst the design of the project enabled me to focus in depth on the experiences of students at a case study university, a wider analysis of policy and provision and its impact on student experience within Welsh universities is needed. Large scale studies (Fuller et al., 2009; Riddell, Tinklin & Wilson, 2005) and smaller research projects (Hall & Tinklin, 1998; Holloway, 2001; Hurst, 1993; O'Connor & Robinson, 1999; Preece, 1995; Vickerman & Blundell, 2010) have to date focused on universities in England and Scotland. Therefore, my first question concerns the impact of devolved political power in Wales on the experiences of disabled students across Welsh higher educational institutions.

My second question stems from the increased focus on disability as an equality issue in the UK (Department for Work and Pensions, 2005; 2010). Whilst the UK government endorsed the social model of disability in *The duty to promote disability equality code of practice* (Disability Rights Commission, 2005, section 1.6), it is important to question the effectiveness of legislation in challenging dominant perceptions about impairment and disability: questions which will also be influenced by changes and priorities in government. My question would seek to evaluate the progress made within higher education in tackling the inequality and the lack of inclusion experienced by disabled students since changes in legislation. Moreover,

118

as part of this questioning process, and set firmly within an equality focus, it is important to identify the value of differing experiences and viewpoints about the relationship between social and individual factors in achieving inclusion.

REFERENCES

Abberley, P. (1992). The significance of the OPCS disability surveys. *Disability, Handicap and Society, 7*(2), 139–155.

Barnes, C. (1991). *Disabled people in Britain and discrimination: A case for anti-discrimination legislation.* London: Hurst & Co.

Barnes, C. (1996). Disability and the myth of the independent researcher. *Disability and Society, 11*(1), 107–110.

Barnes, C., & Mercer, G. (2003). *Disability.* Cambridge: Policy Press.

Beauchamp-Pryor, K. (2008). *A framework for the equality and inclusion of disabled students in higher education.* PhD thesis, Swansea University.

Beauchamp-Pryor, K. (2011). Impairment, cure and identity: 'Where do I fit in?' *Disability and Society, 26*(1), 5–17.

Beauchamp-Pryor, K. (2012a). *Visual impairment and disability: A dual approach towards equality and inclusion in UK policy and provision.* In N. Watson, A. Roulstone & C. Thomas (Eds.), *Routledge handbook of disability studies* (pp. 178–192). Abingdon: Routledge.

Beauchamp-Pryor, K. (2012b). From absent to active voices: Promoting disability equality within higher education. *International Journal of Inclusive Education, 16*(3), 283–295.

Beauchamp-Pryor, K. (2013). *Disabled students in Welsh higher education: A framework for equality and inclusion.* Rotterdam: Sense Publishers

Becker, H. S. (1967). Whose side are we on? *Social Problems, 14,* 239–247.

Campbell, J., & Oliver, M. (1996). *Disability politics: Understanding our past, changing our future.* Abingdon: Routledge.

Davies, C. A. (1999). *Reflexive ethnography: A guide to researching selves and others.* Abingdon: Routledge.

Department for Work and Pensions (DWP). (2005). *The Disability Discrimination Act.* London: HMSO.

Department for Work and Pensions (DWP). (2010). *The Equality Act.* London: HMSO.

Disability Rights Commission (DRC). (2005). *The duty to promote equality: Statutory code of practice.* Stratford-Upon-Avon: DRC.

Drake, R. F. (1996). Charities, authority and disabled people: A qualitative study. *Disability and Society, 11*(1), 5–23.

Duckett, P. S., & Pratt, R. (2001). The researched opinions on research: Visually impaired people and visual impairment research. *Disability and Society, 16*(6), 815–835.

French, S. (Ed.). (1994). *On equal terms working with disabled people.* Oxford: Butterworth-Heinemann Ltd.

Fuller, M., Georgeson, J., Healey, M., Hurst, A., Kelly, K., Riddell, S., Roberts, H., & Weedon, E. (2009). *Improving disabled students' learning: Experiences and outcomes.* Abingdon: Routledge.

Hall, J., & Tinklin, T. (1998). *Students first: The experiences of disabled students in higher education,* Report No.85. Scotland: The Scottish Council for Research in Education.

Hammersley, M. (1995). *The politics of social research.* London: Sage.

Holloway, S. (2001). The experience of higher education from the perspective of disabled students. *Disability and Society, 16*(4), 597–615.

Hunt, P. (1981). Settling accounts with the parasite people: A critique of 'A life apart' by E. J. Miller and G. V. Gwynne. *Disability Challenge, 1,* 37–50. London: UPIAS.

Hurst, A. (1993). *Steps towards graduation: Access to higher education for people with disabilities.* Aldershot: Avebury.

Karl, M. (1995). *Women and empowerment: Participation and decision making.* New Jersey: Zed Brooks.

Kitchin, R. (2000). The researched opinions on research: Disabled people and disability research. *Disability and Society, 15*(1), 25–47.

Luff, D. (1999). Dialogue across the divides: Moments of rapport and power in feminist research with anti-feminist women. *Sociology, 33*(4), 687–703.

Magnus, E. (2006). Disability and higher education – what are the barriers to participation? *Paper presented at the Disability Studies Association Conference,* September 18–20, in Lancaster, United Kingdom.

Morris, J. (1996). *Pride against prejudice.* London: The Women's Press Ltd.

Oakley, A. (1981). Interviewing women: A contradiction in terms. In H. Roberts (Ed.), *Doing feminist research* (pp. 30–61). Abingdon: Routledge.

O'Connor, U., & Robinson, A. (1999). Accession or exclusion? University and the disabled student: A case study of policy and practice. *Higher Education Quarterly, 53*(1), 88–103.

Oliver, M. (1990). *The politics of disablement.* Basingstoke: Macmillan.

Oliver, M. (1992). Changing the social relations of research production? *Disability, Handicap and Society, 7*(2), 101–114.

Oliver, M. (1997). Emancipatory research: Realistic goal or impossible dream? In C. Barnes & G. Mercer (Eds.), *Doing disability research* (pp. 15–31). Leeds: Disability Press.

Oliver, M. (2009). *Understanding disability: From theory to practice* (2nd ed.). Basingstoke: Palgrave Macmillan.

Oliver, M., & Barnes, C. (2012). *The new politics of disablement.* Basingstoke: Palgrave. Macmillan

Preece, J. (1995). Disability and adult education – the consumer view. *Disability and Society, 10*(1), 87–102.

Reimer, J. (1977). Varieties of opportunistic research. *Urban Life, 5*(4), 467–477.

Ribbens, J. (1989). Interviewing – 'an unnatural situation'? *Women's Studies International Forum, 12*(6), 579–92.

Riddell, S., Tinklin, T., & Wilson, A. (2005). *Disabled students in higher education, perspectives on widening access and changing policy.* Abingdon: Routledge.

Rioux, M., & Bach, M. (1994). *Disability is not measles: New paradigms in disability.* Ontario: L'Institut Roeher.

Thomas, C. (1999). *Female forms: Experiencing and understanding disability.* Buckingham: Open University Press.

Thomas, C. (2007). *Sociologies of disability and illness: Contested ideas in disability studies and medical sociology.* Basingstoke: Macmillan.

Vernon, A. (1997). Reflexivity: The dilemmas of researching from the inside. In C. Barnes & G. Mercer (Eds.), *Doing disability research* (pp. 158–176). Leeds: Disability Press.

Vickerman, P., & Blundell, M. (2010). Hearing the voices of disabled students in higher education. *Disability and Society 25*(1), 21–32.

Wheatley, E. (1994). Dances with feminists: Truths, dares and ethnographic stares. *Women's Studies International Forum, 17*(4), 421–423.

SIMONI SYMEONIDOU & KAREN BEAUCHAMP-PRYOR

9. CONCLUDING REMARKS

The final chapter reviews the research experiences presented throughout the volume in an attempt to reflect on important issues raised from the contributors. Focusing on individual experience from the outset contributed to our understanding of those aspects which made the research project meaningful for the researcher and the researched, and important for the field of study.

CONTEXTUALIZING OURSELVES

A critical synthesis of our research projects began with an appreciation of the distinctive features of individual context, which determined the selected research theme and guided a series of decisions, we were called to make, throughout our work.

Importantly, all the stories collected in this volume were informed by the researchers' background experiences and conceptualizations of disability issues, which urged them to engage with disability issues. To begin with, although the social model of disability became a guiding idea of our chosen research topics, each one of us came to know and appreciate it in different ways. Some of us grew up with dominant charitable and medically driven ideas and thus, the acquaintance with the social model of disability was influential in changing predetermined professional and/or research trajectories (for example, D'Alessio, Gavrielidou-Tsielepi). Others were raised to believe that living with disability is 'normal', but yet again, discovering the social model of disability proved liberating and life changing (for example, Reichart). Furthermore, despite our common interest, our background knowledge/studies varied, influencing dramatically the way we sought to link theory to practice, through research. Some of the authors were education graduates with work experience in mainstream class or special education settings (for example, D'Alessio, Gavrielidou-Tsielepi) and were more interested in employing the social model of disability for research exploring the nature and enactment of educational policies. Other authors attempted to explore the place of the social model of disability in a particular work setting they were familiar with or in a legislative framework (for example, Kelly, Reichart) and in these cases, both background knowledge and personal experience of disability were closely related to the choice of topic.

Another important conceptualization is that the contributors of this volume when choosing their research topics were driven by their own personal interests, and influenced by their background studies and their cultural context. For example, one

S. Symeonidou and K. Beauchamp-Pryor (Eds.), Purpose, Process and
Future Direction of Disability Research, 121–126.
© 2013 Sense Publishers. All rights reserved.

important issue was the gap between policy and practice in the implementation of integration and the reproduction of special education under the name of inclusion. The authors from Italy (D'Alessio), Cyprus (Gavrielidou-Tsielepi) and Greece (Spandagou) sensed the dangers inherent in misinterpreting integration policies in their countries and they formulated their research questions to address this issue.

Last but not least, it seems that most of us shared a feeling of gratitude to our supervisors and mentors who introduced us to the social model of disability and at the same time opened new ways of thinking. In many cases, their suggestions to attend a conference or to read a book defined the way many of us finalized our topic. Our own reading and familiarization with the work of key authors in the field (for example, Len Barton, Michael Oliver, Colin Barnes) are remembered as influential and thought provoking.

Overall, all of us as novice researchers, were driven by a desire to contribute to change.

POSITIONING OURSELVES IN THE RESEARCH

Our collection of personal stories suggests that personal identities (shaped by gender, age, ethnicity, impairment, background knowledge/studies, and so forth.) defined our intention of research to a great extent. According to Barton and Clough (1995), the researcher needs to act as a 'critical friend' who is aware of the responsibility and privilege stemming from his/her role and who will endevor not to reproduce the system. Many of us addressed these issues as important for the selection of the research topic and other stages of the research.

Particularly, the fact that some of us were non-disabled researchers raised important issues that we needed to consider regarding our position in the research. The role of non-disabled researchers has been critically debated within disability studies, with concern attached to the lack of shared experience between disabled research participants and non-disabled researchers, and thus the absence of authenticity in the research process (Duckett & Pratt, 2001; Kitchin, 2000). In response, Oliver (2009) asserts that it is a question of control rather than experience. For Barnes and Mercer (1997) because non-disabled researchers live in a disablist society, non-disabled researchers are able to contribute to both disability theory and research. On the one hand, the non-disabled contributors of the volume addressed their concerns regarding their positioning in the research and the right they had to conduct disability research (for example, D'Alessio, Spandagou). On the other hand, the disabled contributors of the volume acknowledged that regardless of their experience of disability, it was not until their acquaintance with the social model of disability that they felt liberated. Being freed by the social model, released them from a fear or anxiety about their right to be involved in the research (for example, Kelly, Reichart).

Our position in the research was further influenced by gender. Some of us explained that being a female researcher influenced our research at some point or determined important methodological decisions regarding the relationship between the researcher and the researched. Thomas (2006) reports on the gendered experience of disability, which was emphasized by disabled feminists and asserts that being a disabled woman can be more difficult than being a disabled man. However, whether researching from a disabled or non-disabled position, most of us acknowledged the fact the gender did play a role at different stages of the research process. For example, Kelly reports that in the presence of a woman researcher, women participants appeared more willing and co-operative than male participants. Furthermore, being a young woman was also reported by some of the researchers as a factor which influenced the way they were accepted by the participants. For example, Spandagou notes that being a woman in her mid-twenties made her look like an undergraduate student and not as a researcher, something which gave her access to information that she might not have gained otherwise.

DECIDING UPON OUR THEORETICAL FRAMEWORK

One shared aspect of our work is that we all placed the social model of disability at the centre of our research, without rejecting the use of broader theoretical frameworks. Such approaches would have been considered problematic a few years ago, as initial discussions about disability research emphasized the need to strictly locate research within the social model. Barnes provides an explanation about why we, as novice researchers, viewed the social model of disability as the guiding ideology of research while at the same time we used it with other theoretical ideas:

A decade ago adopting an overtly social model perspective represented something of a radical departure from conventional wisdom in discussions of disability and dependency. But this is no longer the case. Indeed, in some respects the social model has become the new orthodoxy. (Barnes, 2003, p. 10)

Some of us positioned the research in disability studies and others in inclusive education research and thus, we enriched our theoretical framework with ideas developed in these fields. One important thesis is that researchers operating under the theoretical assumptions of the same field (for example, disability studies) may combine different approaches according to their own conceptualizations of the research project. For example, Kelly explained that she adopted a socialist feminist perspective enhanced by the social model and Foucauldian ideas in order to research the practical influences of the social model in a welfare setting.

RESOLVING METHODOLOGICAL DILEMMAS

A recurring theme in our writings was the discussion around the potential of adopting an emancipatory research methodology or combining other research paradigms that seemed more appropriate in answering our research questions. Oliver (1992) located emancipatory research in the social model of disability and emphasized its relationship with the goals of the disability movement. Stemming from critical theory, emancipatory research became central in discussions around disability research, with disabled activists who strongly believed in the approach (Barnes, 2003; Barnes & Mercer, 1997; Oliver, 1992; 1997; Zarb, 1992; 1997) and others who recognized the importance of alternative research paradigms in conceptualizing both disability and disability politics (Goodley, Lawthom, Clough & Moore, 2004; Shakespeare, 1997; Thomas, 1999). The choice of an emancipatory research approach was a more straightforward option for researchers who experienced disability, although the practicalities of such an approach were appreciated, particularly when working towards doctorial research (for example, Beauchamp-Pryor). Some of us, regardless of whether we were researching from a disabled or non-disabled position, discussed the option of an emancipatory research approach, but decided to adopt different approaches for different reasons. For example, Kelly adopted an ethnographic approach mainly because prior to becoming disabled she used to work for the welfare setting she chose to research. Our choices indicate the value of different types of research in contributing to the emancipation of disabled people in different ways. The examples presented in this volume demonstrated that the divide between 'activism' and 'the academy' (Goodley & Moore, 2000) can be overcome, not necessarily by conducting emancipatory research, but when researchers contribute in furthering conceptualizations of disablement.

DATA COLLECTION, DATA ANALYSIS AND WRITING-UP

Data collection and analysis is a phase full of surprises for novice researchers. During data collection, researchers may end up with more data than they initially expected or they may face barriers in detecting the predefined data. D'Alessio, for example, explained that during data collection, she had to detour from her original goal because the interactions taking place in the research setting pushed her to collect a different kind of data. Allan and Slee (2008) note that data analysis does not follow the neat and tidy process described in textbooks, but is a messy process which novice researchers usually fear. Those of us who tried to interpret qualitative data hoped to construct the best possible story, although at the same time we were aware that our story would be influenced by our viewpoints (for example, Kelly, Reichart). This meant that our final account would not be 'ideology-free', but according to Allan and Slee (2008, p. 98) this is something to be expected in inclusive education research. Writing-up was another important learning experience for us, as we were required to submit a thesis with specific academic requirements within a deadline. For some of the contributors, this took longer than initially anticipated, for different reasons. Those who were within the schedule, confessed hesitation to negotiate the data and other important decisions about the research with respondents because of the restrictions of monitoring a doctoral project (restricted time, organizational issues and inexperience of handling disagreements).

WAS OUR RESEARCH WORTH DOING?

Compiling a doctoral thesis marks the end of a precious learning experience, for which we were all proud of. Some of us felt that our research was extremely important and that it would make an important contribution to the field or to the group/setting researched. As Barton and Clough put it, we had 'a desire to see change take place at the material, institutional, political and attitudinal levels of society' (1995, p. 142). In a similar tone, Allan and Slee warn novice researchers: 'don't expect too much, too soon' (2008, p. 101). Today, some of us feel that perhaps our research was not as influential as we initially expected. However, most of us mention in our accounts that we tried to disseminate our findings, hoping that our work would reach all interested parties. Importantly, some of us can see the usefulness of our research in the long run and we came to believe that our research did have an impact, albeit in other ways we could not anticipate.

A NOTE FOR STUDENTS AND NOVICE RESEARCHERS

The chapters in this book confirm that novice researchers undertaking research leading to a doctoral degree have certain characteristics that differentiate them from experienced researchers: novice researchers are constantly processing new ideas, which they refine by reading and discussing; they think about how best to conduct their study; and they are open to new ideas and ways of conducting research. All these are great features if they are managed for the sake of the research project. If not, novice researchers may face different problems throughout the process. As editors, our engagement with the contributors in this volume (as well as our own research experience) taught us that novice researchers are generally highly motivated and can accomplish high quality research: 'we really (really) wanted to do the research' (Allan & Slee, 2008, p. 97). Our accounts indicate that we experienced our role as researchers in the ways Barton and Clough (1995) describe: the researcher as change agent, researcher as critical friend, accountable researcher, researcher as learner, researcher as teacher and researcher as subject. But no matter how well we performed the researcher's role, we are aware that our research is not the only piece of research out there. We also know that our doctoral theses might be the outcome of inspired work, endless reading, long struggles to float in the data, but our final accounts may entail mistakes, imperfections and compromises. Still, we are all proud of our doctoral work and we are still learning as we research, because surprisingly, our research journeys did not end with the submission of our doctoral theses. We hope that this volume makes a valuable contribution to strengthening the resolve of readers to pursue high quality and meaningful disability research.

REFERENCES

Allan, J., & Slee, R. (2008). *Doing inclusive education research*. Rotterdam: Sense Publishers.
Barnes, C. (2003). What difference a decade makes: Reflections on doing 'emancipatory' disability research. *Disability and Society, 18*(1), 3–17.

Barnes, C., & Mercer, G. (1997.) Breaking the mould? An introduction to doing disability research. In C. Barnes & G. Mercer (Eds.), *Doing disability research* (pp. 1–14). Leeds: The Disability Press.

Barton, L., & Clough, P. (1995). Conclusion: Many urgent voices. In P. Clough, & L. Barton (Eds.), *Making difficulties: Research and the construction of SEN* (pp. 143–147). London: Paul Chapman.

Duckett, P. S., & Pratt, R. (2001). The researched opinions on research: Visually impaired people and visual impairment research. *Disability and Society, 14*(1), 85–101.

Goodley, D., & Moore, M. (2000). Doing disability research: Activist lives and the academy. *Disability and Society, 15*(6), 861–882.

Goodley, D., Lawthom, R., Clough, P., & Moore, M. (2004). *Researching life stories: Method, theory and analyses in a biographical age*. London: RoutledgeFalmer.

Kitchin, R. (2000). The researched opinions on research: Disabled people and disability research. *Disability and Society, 15*(1), 25–47.

Oliver, M. (1992). Changing the social relations of research production. *Disability, Handicap and Society, 7*(2), 101–115.

Oliver, M. (1997). Emancipatory research: Realistic goal or impossible dream? In C. Barnes & G. Mercer (Eds.), *Doing disability research* (pp. 15–31). Leeds: The Disability Press.

Oliver, M. (2009). *Understanding disability: From theory to practice* (2nd ed.). Basingstoke: Palgrave Macmillan.

Shakespeare, T. (1997). Researching disabled sexuality. In C. Barnes & G. Mercer (Eds.), *Doing disability research* (pp. 177–189). Leeds: The Disability Press.

Thomas, C. (1999). *Female forms. Experiencing and understanding disability*. Buckingham: Open University Press.

Thomas, C. (2006). Disability and gender: Reflections on theory and research. *Scandinavian Journal of Disability Research, 8*(2–3), 177–185.

Zarb, G. (1992). On the road to Damascus: First steps towards changing the relations of disability research production. *Disability, Handicap and Society, 7*(2), 125–138.

Zarb, G. (1997). Researching disabling barriers. In C. Barnes & G. Mercer (Eds.), *Doing disability research* (pp. 49–66). Leeds: The Disability Press.

INDEX

Lightning Source UK Ltd.
Milton Keynes UK
UKOW04f1610060314

227689UK00001B/4/P